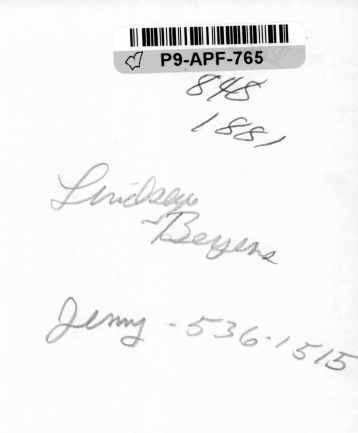

848
(88)

Lindsay
Beyers

Jenny - 536-1515

Other books by Laura Zahn:

"Room at the Inn/Minnesota - Guide to Minnesota's Historic B&Bs, Hotels and Country Inns"
"Room at the Inn/Wisconsin - Guide to Wisconsin's Historic B&Bs and Country Inns"
"WAKE UP & SMELL THE COFFEE - Upper Midwest Edition," Favorite Breakfast and Brunch Recipes from The Upper Midwest's Best Bed & Breakfast Inns
"WAKE UP & SMELL THE COFFEE - Pacific Northwest Edition," Favorite Breakfast and Brunch Recipes from The Pacific Northwest's Best Bed & Breakfast Inns (publication in fall 1990)
"Ride Guide to the Historic Alaska Railroad," with Anita Williams

Room at the Inn/Galena Area -

Guide to Historic B&Bs and Inns
Close to Galena and Dubuque

Laura Zahn

Down to Earth Publications

St. Paul, Minnesota

Published by **Down to Earth Publications**
1426 Sheldon
St. Paul, MN 55108

Distributed by **Voyageur Press**
123 N. Second Street
Stillwater, MN 55082
612-430-2210
1-800-888-9653

Library of Congress Cataloging in Publication Data
Zahn, Laura Claire
          Room at the Inn/Galena Area --
          Guide to Historic B&Bs and Inns Close to Galena and Dubuque
1. Bed and Breakfast Accommodations - Middle West - Directories
TX 907.Z

ISBN 0-939301-61-X (softcover)

Maps by Jim Miller

Photos by Laura Zahn

Pictured on the cover (and art provided by):
        Upper Left Corner - Spring Street Guest House, Galena
        Upper Right Corner - Wisconsin House Stagecoach Inn, Hazel Green, Wis.
        Lower Right Corner - Hellman Guest House, Galena
        Lower Left Corner - Farmer's Home Hotel, Galena

Printing by Malloy Lithographing, Ann Arbor, Michigan

Many people contributed to the publication of this book.

Special thanks to Kathleen Webster, Galena/Jo Daviess County Convention and Visitors Bureau, who helped convince me to do this book and provided information and encouragement, and to the helpful, cheerful co-workers there. Many thanks also to Marilee Harrmann, Dubuque Convention and Visitors Bureau; Daryl Watson at the Galena/Jo Daviess County Historical Society and Museum; Dave Connolly at Cover to Cover Bookstore; Pete Campbell at the Illinois Historic Preservation Agency; Vickie and Terry Cole, Connie and Tom Sola, Flo and Roger Jensen, Rachel Stilson and Merilyn Tommaro, and Ruth and Bill McEllhiney.

Jim Miller, Kristina Ford, Kathy O'Neill, Mary Zahn, Ed Zahn and Leslie Dimond provided invaluable assistance, believe me. And this wasn't the first time, either.

To those innkeepers who re-arranged their schedules, let me use the facilities, fed me, met deadlines, volunteered to help do promotion, included me in their plans, pointed me in the right direction and shared some great stories — you know who you are, and many thanks. I truly could not have done it without you. Nor would I have wanted to.

Contents

❖ Nearby Galena

Not historic (but seems like it)

Welcome to Dubuque.........*Area introduction*............. P. 90

Dubuque Maps.........*Nearby Dubuque and Downtown*.........P. 94

❖ Downtown Dubuque

❖ Nearby Dubuque

Contents Grouped by Category.....................P. 116

Traveling to Galena?......*For more information*........ P. 120

Traveling to Dubuque?.....*For more information*..... P. 121

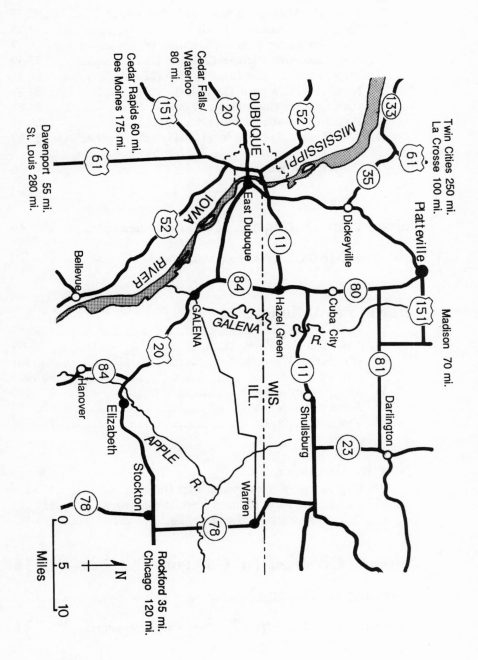

Twin Cities 250 mi.
La Crosse 100 mi.

Cedar Falls/
Waterloo
80 mi.

Cedar Rapids 60 mi.
Des Moines 175 mi.

Davenport 55 mi.
St. Louis 280 mi.

DUBUQUE

MISSISSIPPI

East Dubuque

IOWA

RIVER

Bellevue

Platteville

Dickeyville

Madison 70 mi.

Cuba City

Cuba
R.

Darlington

GALENA

Hazel Green

GALENA

WIS.

ILL.

Shullsburg

Hanover

Elizabeth

APPLE

R.

Stockton

Warren

Rockford 35 mi.
Chicago 120 mi.

N

Miles

0   5   10

8

Introduction

What to Know about this Guide
and Galena Area B&Bs and Inns

The Galena Area is scenic, historically significant and full of recreational activities and opportunities. It's a popular destination, especially for weekend trips.

Just as more people have been "discovering" the Tri-State Area of eastern Iowa, southwestern Wisconsin and northwestern Illinois, more are discovering Bed-and-Breakfast travel. It's appropriate to want to return to a slower pace, if only for overnight, especially in this neck of the woods, where history comes alive.

Galena is "the B&B Capital of the Midwest." Twenty-two historic lodgings within walking distance of downtown are included in this book. There are many others in the surrounding area, and there are many different types of historic lodgings.

How do you find one that's right for you? Read on!

Why is this guide necessary?

This much information isn't available in any other single publication. Many of these establishments are very new and haven't been "written up" in articles or other guides. And most have limited advertising or public relations budgets.

Also, many travelers don't know what B&Bs or country inns are, and some municipalities are giving prospective innkeepers a tremendously hard time because of ignorance. Perhaps this book will serve as an educational tool to spread the good news — this is a *great* way to travel and a tourism asset in every community.

What is a "B&B?"

B&B stands for "Bed and Breakfast." For years, travelers to Europe have enjoyed inexpensive accommodations in the extra bedroom of a local family's home. They found that B&Bs not only saved money and provided lodging in out-of-the-way places, but were a great way to meet friendly local people.

To say B&Bs are catching on in America is a whopper of an understatement. Both coasts are loaded with them, and at least two national magazines are devoted to them. In the Midwest, historic B&Bs are not necessarily economical, but they remain a good way to meet neighbors and are much different than a motel or hotel.

The Illinois definition of a B&B (which a number of Galena innkeepers authored, including Judy Green of the Aldrich Guest House and Connie Sola of Comfort Guest House) means the facility has five guest rooms or less, is owner or manager-occupied, and breakfast is the only meal which can be prepared and served. Innkeepers must pass a health department food-handling course.

In addition, the city of Galena adds more stringent restrictions, including prohibiting working fireplaces in guest rooms and requiring sophisticated smoke detecting systems, for instance. Every year, the city conducts individual fire, health and building inspections.

In Iowa, B&Bs that have one or two guest rooms are not required to be licensed by the state. With three or more guest rooms, a hotel/motel license is needed, according to a spokeswoman for the Iowa B&B Association, which has additional safety and health standards. Nine or fewer guest rooms is considered a "B&B inn."

The City of Dubuque has additional restrictions to state law, requiring, for instance, that B&Bs be five guest rooms or less and owner-occupied. B&Bs are allowed to serve meals to overnight guests only.

In Wisconsin, a 1990 law defines a B&B as an owner-occupied place of lodging with eight guest rooms or less (increased from four). The only meal which can be served to guests is breakfast. Inns with more than eight guest rooms or which cook and serve other meals have to apply for motel/hotel, restaurant or other licenses.

Variety is the spice of life

Galena has much more to offer than a "typical" B&B, if there is such a thing. There are B&Bs in grand mansions and in more modest homes. There are ones which have been painstakingly restored, accurate to each detail. There are others in the process of restoration. Some are not completely restored, and are looked at by their owners as being comfortable homes, not photo-spreads in "Architectural Digest" or "Country Home." B&Bs are often favored because innkeepers are around to chat or to ask for recommendations about restaurants and sightseeing.

There are historic country inns, bigger than B&Bs, possibly with more amenities and with more privacy, and with restaurant facilities on the premises.

There is one historic hotel, with an elevator, dining rooms, meeting rooms and all the hotel conveniences, including a parking ramp.

Then there are some other "variations." There are private cottages, suites and apartments that may include stocked kitchen facilities, a whirlpool, a fireplace and a baby crib. These are good for families (many B&Bs will not accept children because they can disturb other guests or break antiques) and friends traveling together, or for private, romantic getaways.

Remember that with the privacy of an inn, hotel, cottage or suite comes less personal attention by innkeepers.

In Dubuque, the downtown B&Bs are all in huge historic homes. Indeed, Dubuque allows B&Bs only in its historic districts. Nearby are a B&B on a non-working farm and a private guest cottage. The B&B in East Dubuque is in the town's grandest home.

B&Bs are popular with Galena area travelers

Most folks come to Galena to revel in its preservation and restoration efforts and to admire the architecture. It's only natural, then, to want to stay in an historic building.

B&Bs in Galena are very busy June through October. Try to call for reservations well in advance. Within a few weeks or days of your stay, you can call the Galena/Jo Daviess County Convention and Visitors Bureau, and someone there will tell you which member inns have vacancies on your night (1-800-747-9377). The same goes during the summer for the Dubuque Convention and Visitors Bureau (1-800-798-4748). Remember that not all inns in this book are members; don't assume that all of them are filled if the CVBs say their members are.

The popularity of B&Bs in "peak season" means that many innkeepers require a two-night minimum stay on weekends (and/or a three-night minimum on holidays, such as the Fourth of July or Labor Day). That means that on a weekend, you must stay *both* Friday and Saturday *or* Saturday and Sunday nights at whatever the weekend rate is per night.

Innkeepers do this simply because if they accept your reservation for Saturday night only, they often turn down later callers who want to reserve that room for Friday *and* Saturday or Saturday *and* Sunday. Sometimes innkeepers aren't able to fill a single night on a Friday, so they end up losing that income. Unfortunately, that restriction prohibits weekenders from the Twin Cities or St. Louis who aren't able to drive in at a reasonable hour after work on Friday. However, if you are looking for reservations for only a week ahead of your visit, call anyway — the rooms that aren't sold for two nights are sold for one night as the weekend draws nearer.

What to expect at a B&B

Some additional typical characteristics of a B&B include shared bathrooms and other rooms, like a den or dining room, and breakfast is included in the room rate. It's common for guests to find themselves talking with other guests and the hosts in the living room at night, making arrangements to have dinner together, and sharing travel tips as they pass the breakfast platter the next morning.

That won't happen in a motel or hotel room. And, unlike motels or hotels, each B&B is different. Most are cozy and homey. Guests are, after all, sharing someone's home, which means guests really are guests and should act as such. Meeting the owners is part of the personalized service.

Don't be afraid to try a B&B during your next trip or getaway. And, if the first one isn't quite what you had envisioned, do try another -- they are all very different. To avoid disappointment, know your tastes and expectations and then find out what the place offers. This book is designed to help you find lodging that suits you.

What is a country inn?

A country inn doesn't have to be in the country. What makes it "country" is more its atmosphere and size. It's larger than a B&B but smaller than a hotel. A country inn has some of the personal atmosphere of a B&B with some of the privacy of a hotel. Some amenities, like phones or TVs in the room, are more common than in B&Bs. Breakfast may or may not be included in the room rate. Inns may be more likely to serve meals other than breakfast, and innkeepers may be more able to put on weddings or other private parties. Both at B&Bs and at country inns, expect no bellhop, no elevator and no room service.

About the innkeepers

Innkeepers often have many motivations for opening their homes, or for renovating a building as a lodging facility. If you have strong ideas about the type of experience you want, identify your needs, then read until you find a place to match.

For example, if you want to be able to sit in the innkeeper's living room and munch a homemade cookie with milk, but you don't give two hoots about the decor or the privacy, read until you find a place that sounds like this kind of experience. If you want a romantic overnight and you don't want to eat breakfast with other guests, read until you find a place that sounds like this. If you have a strong interest in Victorian decor and preservation/re-construction, read until you find an innkeeper with the background and skills about which you'd like to hear.

To Whirlpool or Not to Whirlpool

Many innkeepers in historic homes believe that whirlpool spas, color TVs, phones in the room and other amenities are not in keeping with the notion of stepping back into the era in which the home was built.

Nevertheless, many travelers don't seem to care if they are getting an "authentic B&B experience" and want those extras anyway. Some innkeepers have installed them. Others would prefer that you go elsewhere if you require those amenities. Read descriptions carefully. The "Contents Grouped by Category" at the back of this book has categories for whirlpool and fireplace rooms.

Suggestions for being a good guest

Most people who choose to travel this way are wonderful folks: quiet, easy-going and honest. It's rare, innkeepers say, to have a check bounce or find a towel missing. Still, here are a few hints that will ingratiate you with innkeepers.

The point, of course, is to feel at home. But remember it is someone else's home, and you are a guest. Don't call for reservations at midnight. Don't tie up their phone. Be thoughtful of other guests, especially if you smoke or are sharing bathrooms. Hosts will often provide information on local activities, but they are not personal tour guides.

Remember, if you don't show up for your room and the innkeeper can't re-rent it (quite likely, since few B&Bs take "walk ins" and instead depend on advance reservations), he or she may lose a half or a quarter of that night's income. So do keep in touch if plans change.

If you honestly think you are a good guest when you visit friends or relatives, and you *enjoy* staying in someone else's home, you will be a good B&B/inn traveler.

Who was selected to be included in this book?

First of all, only historic structures were included. "Historic" is defined as 50 years or older and, hopefully, of some local historic significance. Several of the structures included in this guide are listed on the National Register of Historic Places, and all of them have interesting pasts.

Secondly, innkeepers were told that their place needed to "feel" historic both inside and out. The history could be carried inside through Early American, Victorian or "country" decor or use of antiques or reproductions.

Therefore, historic homes or buildings which have been completely modernized and then turned into B&Bs were not included. Some historic B&Bs which had a mix of modern and antique furniture were noted. That should be a red flag to those who expect flawless decor.

Unlike many guides, which make money both from readers buying the book and from innkeepers paying to be included, no one paid to be in this book. This book is intended to provide credible information for the benefit of readers/travelers, not as an advertising vehicle for innkeepers. Not all historic B&Bs or inns were selected for inclusion (see below).

Each facility included was personally visited by the author. Please do not think this counts as any kind of "inspection," as cleanliness and other aspects of service may vary. Cleanliness or other concerns about the way business is conducted should be reported to health, business and tourism officials.

Many of the innkeepers whose lodgings were selected for inclusion have spent long hours and lots of money in restoration, renovation and redecoration. Some have spent considerably less on all of the above. Which brings us to...

Opinion, or "Just the facts, ma'am?"

This book is intended as a guide to provide information, not a be-all-and-end-all rating service. In most cases, if facilities met the above criteria, they were included. The writing was intended to satisfy readers' interests on the historic nature of the home, who the innkeepers are, and why and how they got into innkeeping. It also was designed simply to describe the facilities of the B&B or inn. Readers can make their own choices according to their own tastes and preferences. Readers are advised to pay careful attention to descriptions.

Who is not included?

Not all historic lodgings were included. The reasons varied. Two historic structures were left out because they did not fit the above criteria. One was not included because it did not seem to be the type of place which the audience of this book would want to visit, for several reasons, including having only 2.5 baths for 10 guest rooms (potentially 20 guests). For another, information could not be obtained. Doubtless, some were left out because the author was not aware of them.

Please note that it's possible that a facility described in this book has been sold and is no longer operating as a B&B or has new owners who do things differently. At the time of this printing, four of the 41 places were on the market, to the publisher's knowledge.

Part of the fun of traveling this way is getting to know the hosts. Therefore, reservation services have not been included. Arrangements can be made directly with each of the innkeepers featured in this guide; travelers are encouraged to do so.

What readers should know about...

...Descriptions: For each facility, a short feature was written about the history of the inn, renovation or restoration efforts, and the innkeepers themselves. This was designed to give interesting background information about the facility and the people who run it, since every place has its own story. Historical information was provided by the innkeepers and the Galena/JoDaviess County Historical Society.

...Rooms: The number of rooms and some examples of decor and bathroom arrangements are explained. Please ask innkeepers for more complete information.

...Rates: Rates are current for all of 1990, in most cases. If in doubt, assume about 5 percent increase per year. **All rates are subject to change**, however, and please do not call innkeepers nasty names if their rates have gone up.

B&Bs rates in the Galena area are not cheap. Substantial discounts (sometimes more than 25 percent off) can be obtained by traveling midweek or offseason .

Remember, rates often have little in common with what guests will get at area hotels or motels for the same rate. Here's a very general breakdown on what guests might get for their money:

$85 and up - Expect extra-special rooms. For this amount, you should get the honeymoon suite with a whirlpool and/or fireplace, an unparalleled view, candies on the pillow at night, and/or a gourmet breakfast. The inns in this price range have probably had major renovation and expert decoration, perhaps with designer linens or handmade quilts, for example. Privacy is the norm here.

$50 - $80 - These are considered "mid-priced lodgings" in the B&B industry. A $50 room may be worth every bit as much as the higher priced, except for one thing (no whirlpool or view, or it has a shared bath, or a tub only). Maybe the B&B is located slightly out of town or in a town which won't support higher rates.

Unfortunately, it's no longer true that you can always expect tasteful decor and comfortable furnishings in this price range. Frankly, some of these places have not been redecorated or have not been done well. Read descriptions carefully to see what matches your tastes and expectations.

These B&Bs are most likely where you'll find the more traditional "B&B experience" — places that are smaller and where opportunities are greater to sit on the porch swing and talk with other guests or the owners, or have them sit down at the breakfast table with you.

$45 and Under - Hardly any room in the Galena area is available for less than $45. This price range means that a particular room is small, or the B&B is in an out-of-the-way spot that doesn't draw big tourism dollars. Other times it's because the B&B is run by people who believe in keeping the price low, or they find themselves financially able to do so. The low price doesn't mean the place isn't clean or otherwise perfectly OK.

Other times, it's cheaper because relatively little money has been put into converting the home into a B&B. That means shared baths, perhaps rugs instead of carpeting, painted walls instead of wallpapered, or the living room has dad's easy chair instead of chintz-covered designer furniture. Again, read descriptions carefully to see what matches your tastes and expectations.

...Tax: In Illinois, sales tax is 6 percent. There's an additional 3 percent tax in JoDaviess County, for 9 percent total. It may go up to 9.5 percent if a "toilet tax" to fund a public restroom downtown passes (so to speak).

In Iowa, sales tax is 4 percent, plus an additional 5 percent "hotel/motel" tax, for a total of 9 percent.

In addition to Wisconsin sales tax of 5 percent, many municipalities levy a "bed tax" or "room tax," which overnight lodging facilities must charge. Commonly, that money is used to promote the community. Up to 10 percent total tax added to your bill in some communities.

...Shared baths: Can we talk? Let's be frank. Don't shy away from a place because you have to share a bathroom. It's not like you're traveling in Mexico and you need to spend half your vacation in there.

Some people envision "shared bath" very literally, as if there were five or six people in there all at once. Not the case, of course, and most often there are only two or three rooms sharing. And some of those might not be rented, in which case you'll end up with a private bath, anyway. *The key is how many people will be sharing the bath.*

Of course, if the thought of someone else's germs in the shower makes your skin crawl, this is not a good option for you. But "shared bath" doesn't have to mean "dirty bath." Most B&B guests are clean-cut folks who will keep the bathroom pretty clean, especially if they know someone else is using it.

If you share, simply be courteous of other guests (translation: if you walk around naked at home, please throw on a robe here). If the bathroom door is shut, don't go in. Also, a sink in the bedroom can be a big help; then teeth can be brushed without having to get in the shared bathroom.

...Meals: Breakfast is included in the room rate at B&Bs and most inns. Coffee, tea, milk and juice should be expected to be provided and are not listed here. Otherwise, breakfast varies from a roll set out on a platter in the hallway to be eaten in one's room to a three-course homemade breakfast served in the dining room on fine china and linens. When a homemade breakfast is offered, special diets almost always can be accommodated if enough advance notice is given.

...Smoking: As more non-smokers are asserting themselves, more innkeepers are feeling less guilty and "just say no." Some inns allow smoking outside on porches only. Others don't want smokers to bother other guests, so smoking is allowed only in the private guest rooms. Still others don't want the liability of people smoking in bed and don't allow it in guest rooms. Some fire regulations limit where guests can smoke.

If smoking is allowed and it bothers you, you may wish to ask innkeepers if they personally smoke and in what particular areas of the house smoking is allowed. Whenever possible, it has been noted in this section when innkeepers smoke — though some are not happy about it. It's really not a problem in the summer, if windows are open, and in big houses, but it does make a big difference to non-smokers who visit in the winter and want to enjoy the home's public areas.

...Children: While some establishments welcome children, others are designed as weekend or special-event adult getaways. They are not set up for children of any age who may disturb other guests. Others simply don't have cribs or child-proof furnishings. Some may accept older children but require renting a separate room for them.

On the other hand, even places that say "no children" may make an exception when they have room available and no other guests, so it doesn't hurt to ask.

...Pets: Even fewer lodgings will accept pets than will accept children. Still, there are those that will. Some innkeepers will make arrangements for your pet at a local kennel at your request.

Also, note that many innkeepers have their own pets, most of which are friendly animals who are thrilled to welcome guests. Many innkeepers do not allow their pets in the guest rooms; since innkeepers usually clean daily and vacuum several times a week, allergies often are not a problem.

...Handicapped Access: Few historic buildings are equipped for wheelchair access by having ramps, elevators, wide doorways or bathroom fixtures. Still, it is important to note the few which do.

...Air Conditioning (A/C): Central or window units are designated.

...Other/Group Uses: Nearly every B&B will give you a price break for "whole house" rental for reunions, for instance. Other specialties are noted here.

...Nearby: It is assumed that the major attraction in Galena is Main Street for its restaurants, shopping, walking tour and historic sites. See the "Welcome to Galena" and "Welcome to Dubuque" introductions to the Galena and Dubuque sections for more information on attractions.

Many innkeepers keep brochures or local guides and local restaurant menus on hand for guests, and are happy to make recommendations and provide directions.

For more information before leaving home, contact the Convention and Visitors Bureau at your destination.

❖ Information about the **Galena/JoDaviess County Convention and Visitors Bureau** is listed on page 120.
❖ Information about the **Dubuque Convention and Visitors Bureau** is listed on page 121.

...Location: The directions probably won't be helpful unless or until you are looking at a map or are in town trying to find the place.

...Deposit: Most innkeepers want a deposit to hold advance reservations. Ask about cancellation policies when making the reservation.

...Payment: Nearly every innkeeper will accept personal checks, so credit cards are not necessary. Small B&Bs often cannot afford the service charges tacked on by credit card companies, so they prefer to operate on a cash basis. However, more are offering the convenience of credit card payment or, at least, deposit confirmation.

For more information, simply ask! This book provides an introduction to the innkeepers. Just pick up the phone and call. They'll be happy to help you.

Happy traveling!

The DeSoto House Hotel was the center of the Aug. 18, 1865, celebration on Main Street that drew an estimated 25,000 people when General Ulysses S. Grant returned from the Civil War. The DeSoto House, built in 1855 at a cost of $85,000, had its top two stories removed in 1880. It is featured on pages 42-43. (Photo courtesy of the Alfred W. Mueller Collection, Illinois Historic Preservation Agency)

Welcome to Galena

Galena's motto is "the town that time forgot." Garrison Keillor, about his mythical Lake Wobegon, Minn., always added, "the decades could not improve."

So it is with Galena today. A *real* town. A town that has two foundries, a Kraft Swiss cheese plant, good schools, active civic and religious groups. It enjoys the incredible time-warp privilege of supporting both a McDonalds and a blacksmith shop right within two miles of each other.

Today the town has only 4,000 residents and cannot rival its 1840-50s population of four times that. But Galena's time once again has come.

Galena's original boom began in the 1820s with the mining of lead in the surrounding hills. About 1845, lead mining and smelting reached their peak, and the need for a fine hotel resulted in the building of The DeSoto House in 1855.

All Mississippi River traffic between St. Louis and Fort Snelling (near St. Paul) stopped in Galena, and as many as 18 steamboats tied up at the Galena River levee at once. Only St. Louis and New Orleans claimed more resident steamboat owners at the time. Ulysses S. Grant arrived in 1860 on a steamboat to make Galena his home. Five years later, at The DeSoto House, the General was heralded upon his return from the Civil War.

After the end of the Civil War, the arrival of the Illinois Central Railroad (reducing river traffic), the silting in of the Galena River (it was once three times as wide and three times as deep as it is now), and other factors, Galena fell into an economic depression so severe that most residents and merchants could not afford to tear down existing buildings to replace them. In the 1960s, many Chicago-area artists and residents re-discovered Galena, bought the buildings at incredibly low prices, and began restoration. Such buildings, which line the main streets and the now-shallow river, are the prized possessions of the 4,000 residents and "weekenders" from Chicago, or others who opened stores and restored historic buildings.

Now Galena is booming again. Galena is Illinois' second most popular attraction after Springfield; Chicago wasn't counted. Officials estimate 1.5 million people visit Galena every year.

If you love old houses, Galena is going to knock your socks off. A variety of architectural styles are visible in every direction. Sixty-three historic buildings are listed on walking tours, and you can tour President Ulysses Grant's house and other historic mansions.

Galena's downtown, on the riverbank, is like walking into a time warp, with busy antique and gift stores, restaurants, a market house and a winery, which offers tasting and tours.

And that is why people come to Galena. The main street appears as if it was frozen in the 19th century, with shop after shop of beautifully restored storefronts for 10 blocks. The side streets are full of beautiful old homes with interesting architectural styles of the period in which they originally were constructed. Many of them, too, have been restored to their original (or, one gets the sense, better) splendor. The entire downtown is an historic district, and 85 percent of the town is listed in the National Register of Historic Places.

Felt, Gear, Chetlain, DeZoya, Avery, Harris, Snyder, Hellman, Craig, Speier, Stillman, and others. These were the town founders, politicians, the merchants, the steamboat captains, the miners, the war heros, the entrepreneurs that participated in an exciting time in history in Galena. And it is their homes that now are open as B&Bs to welcome travelers who come to recapture a feeling of that past.

But buildings do not a town make. People do.

I was privileged to spend some time in Galena in January 1990 while writing this book.

People said "hello" to me on the street, and waved at me from their cars (using all their fingers).

At the Steakburger Inn — known locally as "Pete's," where a bowl of shrimp cheese chowder and a yummy piece of homemade peach pie (which they can't warm up because they don't have a microwave) came to $2.96 — the lunchtime occupants of the four tables and 15-or-so stools all knew each other.

At another restaurant (also where everyone one was on a first-name basis), the lone waitress was overworked. So a diner got up, poured coffee for his table, and then poured it for everybody else, too. And everyone laughed about it.

In the post office, where I once waited in a remarkably short line, the woman in front of me was a local businessperson who was going to do a bulk mailing. "Bring them in," the post office clerk told her, "and we'll show you how to do it." *Show* how to do it? Did she mean *actually help?* How wonderful (and how rare) to hear a government employee offer to do something extra for somebody. The post office clerk talked as if she and the businesswoman were neighbors. In a town this size, they might very well be.

By the second week, I was running into people I knew on the street and in the library. I *felt* like we were neighbors.

There really is something wonderful about a small town.

And there is something particularly wonderful about Galena, where merchants and homeowners and entrepreneurs have seen the potential for what their town could be, if it was restored, and then have acted on it. (How many other architecturally-blessed small American towns have neither the vision nor the energy? And how many other small towns can claim two historic downtown walking tours featuring a total of 63 historic buildings on essentially two streets?)

Of course, I do not choose to go to Galena in the heat and humidity of mid-summer, nor among the crowds of "leaf peepers" looking for a fall weekend getaway. Too many people in too small a space completely ruin the "experience." Most visitors come June through October. I advise others to go "off season" in cool weather.

Here are some other reasons to visit Galena:

Main Street Shopping/Restaurants - There are about 10 blocks of stores, including antique and gift shops. Restaurants are rated highly, especially the Kingston Inn (with singing waitstaff) and Silver Annie's (I also liked the Steakburger Inn and Fran's Cafe, out the road toward Dubuque, for old-time cafe food). Yes, shops are open on Sundays, year 'round.

Historical Museum - at 211 S. Bench St. is open 9 a.m. - 4:30 p.m. Open all year except Thanksgiving, Christmas and New Year's Day, and costs adults $2.50. There are exhibits, an hourly video, a gift shop and restrooms.

Old Market House - at 423 N. Commerce is a state historic site with a video every 30 minutes and exhibits on history and architecture. It also has restrooms, is open 362 days a year 9 a.m. - noon and 1-5 p.m., and admission is free!

Grant's House - at 500 Bouthiller St. (in East Galena) is a state historic site. Admission is free, and it's open 9 a.m. - 5 p.m. daily except for Thanksgiving, Christmas and New Year's Day. Tour guides show you through the home, which is furnished with period pieces and items belonging to the Grants.

Historical/Architectural Walking Tours - Pick up a brochure at the Depot Visitors Center in East Galena or elsewhere in town on these two do-it-yourself walking tours. Tour A has 37 buildings in eight blocks; Tour B has 16 buildings in 7 blocks. Both tours basically are on Main and Bench streets.

Galena Cellars Winery - Located at 515 S. Main in a former granary, this is now the flagship winery of the Christina Lawlor family. Tours cost $1 and are offered daily June through October and weekends November through May. (People can "taste" all year long.) Check tour times when you get to town. If you miss the tour, the fruit and table wines are for sale in the local grocery stores.

Public House Tours - Twice a year, four different homes in town are open for a benefit house tour. Ask the Convention and Visitors Bureau folks if that will be going on when you're in town and how to get tickets (it often includes one or more B&B). Private mansions also are open for public tours at about $2.50 per person.

Skiing - Ski season is December through February (some say Thanksgiving through St. Patrick's Day). Downhill skiing is at Chestnut Mountain Resort, where slopes are on the Mississippi River bluffs. X-c skiing is available at Eagle Ridge Inn and Resort in the Galena Territory. Both are within 15 minute drives of downtown.

Antiquing, artists studios and shops, cheese plants, picnicking, guided town tours - Through Jo Daviess County. Get thee to the Depot Visitor Center, or call 1-800-747-9377.

Riverboat Gambling - Sorry, that's on the Mississippi, not the Galena River. But Dubuque is supposed to "get" it in April 1991, and East Dubuque, Illinois, may have it earlier in January 1991. See the "Welcome to Dubuque" section.

Driving Times, depending on destination, speed and road conditions (and how many times you stop!) to Galena from:

Chicago - 3 to 4 hours
Minneapolis-St. Paul - 5 to 6 hours
St. Louis - 6 to 7 hours
Madison - 90 minutes
Milwaukee - 3 to 4 hours
Dubuque - 20 minutes
House on the Rock (near Spring Green) - 1 hour
Amana Colonies - 90 minutes
Mineral Point, Wis. - 1 hour

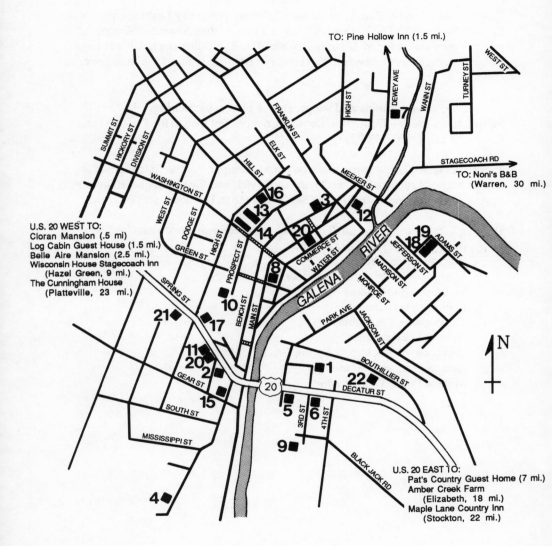

TO: Pine Hollow Inn (1.5 mi.)

STAGECOACH RD

TO: Noni's B&B
(Warren, 30 mi.)

U.S. 20 WEST TO:
Cloran Mansion (.5 mi)
Log Cabin Guest House (1.5 mi.)
Belle Aire Mansion (2.5 mi.)
Wisconsin House Stagecoach Inn
    (Hazel Green, 9 mi.)
The Cunningham House
    (Platteville, 23 mi.)

U.S. 20 EAST TO:
Pat's Country Guest Home (7 mi.)
Amber Creek Farm
    (Elizabeth, 18 mi.)
Maple Lane Country Inn
    (Stockton, 22 mi.)

N

❖ Downtown Galena (or within walking distance)

Directions are posted on the map to inns listed in the "Nearby Galena" section.

Aldrich Guest House

900 Third St.
Galena, IL 61036
815-777-3323

Owner/Operator:
Judy Green

In 1845, State Rep. Cyrus Aldrich built a one-room, 1-1/2 story brick house. Both were destined for bigger things. Aldrich later moved to Minneapolis, where he became a U.S. senator and after whom Aldrich Avenue is named. The house also went on to become one of the grandest in Galena.

A major addition was made in 1853 by J.R. Jones. Jones was appointed Minister to Belgium in 1869 by President U. S. Grant, his friend. An Italianate addition was put on in the 1880s by Robert McClellan, a state senator and lawyer. Grant, whom McClellan supported, often was hosted in the double parlor.

Ownership changed over the years, and the house once was used as club house for a lawn bowling club. It was restored in 1984 and opened as a B&B.

About the same time the plumbing was being replaced, Judy Green was contemplating a career change after 14 years in the New York publishing industry. "I had no idea what I wanted to do, but I knew I didn't want to work for another big corporation again." She saw an ad in the New York Times business section for a seminar for prospective B&B owners. "I had stayed in B&Bs but had never thought of running one." She signed up for the seminar, then looked for a B&B.

"I knew about Galena because I grew up in Chicago." She bought the B&B in December 1985, arriving with only a few pieces of furniture. Seven "frantic" weeks later, she was open for Valentine's Day.

Guests may enjoy the grand piano, stereo and fireplace in the front parlor and the big screened side porch with wicker furniture and swing. There are no TVs.

Rooms and Rates: Five - All upstairs. Aldrich Room is original loft, has wood plank floors, queen antique bed, bath with clawfoot tub/shower - $79. McClellan Room has queen antique carved bed, bay window with sitting area, done in mauve, bath has clawfoot tub/shower and pull-chain toilet - $89. Crowe's Nest has queen antique walnut bed, beige floral wallpaper (rented as suite with McClellan Room or shares bath with Jones Room) - $69. Jones Room has queen white iron bed, twin white iron bed, done in medium green mini-print wallpaper; shares bath downstairs; bath has shower only - $69. Reynolds Room has queen brass bed and twin bed, antique oak furniture, done in mint green, bath with tub/shower - $85. Rates are double; single, $5 less. Weekdays, $10 less. Seniors, $5 less. Two-night minimum stay required most weekends. Add tax.

Meals: Breakfast is served in the dining room 8:30-9:30. It may include fresh fruit salad, homemade muffins or coffeecake, and an entree such as pancakes, French toast, quiche or an egg dish.

Dates Open: Year 'round

Smoking: Living room or porch only

Children: Over 6

Pets: No

Handicapped Access: No

A/C: Central

Other/Group Uses: Small meetings with social hour, catered meals. One-day seminars of up to 20.

Location: Located in East Galena. From Highway 20, turn north on Third Street; B&B is at end of block. Main Street, 3 blocks.

Deposit: First night's lodging or confirmation by credit card

Payment: Cash, personal or traveler's checks, VISA, MasterCard, AMEX or Discover

Avery Guest House

606 S. Prospect St.
Galena, IL 61036
815-777-3883

Owners/Operators:
Flo and Roger Jensen

Over its long life, this hillside home has enjoyed ownership by several prominent Galena families. It is named after the family that owned it for more than 40 years, from 1881 to 1923.

"Major Avery," as the patriarch was known, was, indeed, a Civil War major, and he often led town parades dressed in his military uniform. But he was more than a war-time figure. He served as postmaster, was president of the school board, and founded a couple of manufacturing companies in town. In 1887, one of his daughters was married in the home to a member of the Felt family (from the house now known as Felt Manor Guest House). Her wedding dress is on display at the Historical Museum on Bench Street.

About the time Averys bought the house, a second wing was added. Historic photos show that a stairway stretched up the hillside from Spring Street, a boon to later owners who operated their gas station at the base of the hill.

Another later owner, Mable Virtue, turned the home into a boarding house in the late 1950s. Her sister donated Galena's water park on the east edge of town, and her grandson lived in the house until he sold it to Flo and Roger Jensen in 1986.

"We moved in just before the fall house tour and opened three days later," said Roger, who had retired from aerospace engineering at Lockheed in Burbank, Calif., to Green Lake, Wis. He and Flo are native Illinoisans who wanted to be closer to their daughter and grandchildren living in Galena.

Guests have use of a large, paneled living room with modern furniture, a piano for singalongs, games and a library with TV. The back porch looks over the hill and has a swing and picnic table, and a children's play house is in the yard.

Rooms and Rates: Four - All upstairs with queen beds and ceiling fans. Room 1 has peach iron bed, braided rugs, floral green and rose wallpaper. Room 2 has small second room for a baby's bed, is done in beige, gold and white. 1 and 2 share a bath with clawfoot tub/shower. Room 3 has candystriped carpet, handmade star quilt, carved maple headboard, and beige, blue and peach wallpaper. Room 4 has a carved headboard and a twin four-poster bed, blue floral wallpaper and a view of the Steamboat House and Fulton Brewery. 3 and 4 share a modern bath with tub/shower. $45 weekdays, $55 weekends, $5 less for second night. Rate is double; single, $5 less. Two-night minimum required most weekends. Add tax.

Meals: Continental breakfast is served in the dining room 8-9. It may include bran muffins or Kaiser rolls, homemade coffeecake or a sweet bread, cheese plate and a fresh fruit bowl.

Dates Open: Year 'round

Smoking: Outdoors only

Children: Yes (toys available)

Pets: No

Handicapped Access: No

A/C: Window units

Other/Group Uses: Reunions or retreats, meetings of 15 or less.

Location: Turn south on Prospect at the Fulton Brewery corner, one block from the stop light on Main Street.

Deposit: First night's lodging or confirmation by credit card

Payment: Cash, personal or traveler's checks, VISA, MasterCard or AMEX

Brierwreath Manor B&B

216 N. Bench St.
Galena, IL 61036
815-777-0608

Owners/Operators:
Lyn and Mike Cook

This white Queen Anne home with a large wrap-around porch was literally built on top of a limestone quarry. The house is on a limestone ledge and to construct the basement, limestone had to be blasted out and carried away.

But James Hudson, the local butcher and patriarch of a large family, went ahead and built this huge home in 1884. Hudson, like other Galenians, fought in the Civil War, sustaining a wound; his brother and father were killed.

Only two other families owned the home before Cooks bought it in 1988. One was Mayor Frank Einsweiler, who sold it to them when he retired after 15 years in office. "He was really important in bringing Galena back," said Lyn.

Lyn and Mike were no strangers to Galena. "We had lived here in the early 70s and we had both our sons here," she said. But there were no full-time jobs, and they returned to the Chicago suburbs, close to her sister, Lorraine Svec. Then, one April, Lyn and Mike invited Svecs on a getaway weekend to Galena. "Lorraine wanted to look for a B&B. She'd been to a seminar on running a B&B and B&B was all I heard for three weeks before that," Lyn said.

Before the weekend was over, Lorraine had decided to purchase the Belle Aire Mansion and Lyn and Mike were talked into selling their house and moving in as partners. "I've always liked the work," Lyn said. She also had demanding cooking experience, earned by feeding her teenage sons and their friends on weekends.

Cooks and Svecs were partners for a year and then Cooks moved into Brierwreath. "It's kind of like being paid for being a mom," Lyn explained. She mothers guests by providing beverages upstairs early in the morning. Guests admire her cut glass, talk to the cockateil, enjoy the front porch, and have their own parlor with TV, a recliner, gold sculptured carpet and some modern furniture.

Rooms and Rates: Three - All upstairs with ceiling fans and private baths. Mayor's Room has double bed, some modern furniture and sofa, done in rose, bath with shower only. Country Charms Suite has queen bed, done in roses and greens, sitting room with blue country sofa sleeper, bath with tub/shower. Far East Suite has queen bed, sitting room with daybed, large oriental fan on wall, beige walls and green sculptured carpet, bath in gold with French Provincial cabinets, clawfoot tub, separate shower. $75 weekends, $65 weekdays. Rate is double; single, $5 less. Seniors, $5 less. Two-night minimum stay required holiday weekends. Add tax.

Meals: Breakfast is served in the dining room 8-9:30. It may include fresh fruit, muffins, ham, bacon or sausage, and apple-cinnamon French toast. Lyn sometimes makes homemade donuts on Sundays.

Dates Open: Year 'round

Children: "Prefer not"

Handicapped Access: No

Other/Group Uses: No

Smoking: Outside only

Pets: No

A/C: Central

Location: Bench Street runs parallel to Main Street, 1 block up the hill from shops and restaurants.

Deposit: Confirmation by credit card

Payment: Cash, personal or traveler's checks only

Captain Gear Guest House

1000 S. Bench St.
Galena, IL 61036
815-777-0222

Owner/Operator:
Alyce A. Green

Many visitors who've been to Galena before don't know this grand home even exists. It's located almost at the south end of Bench Street, after the pavement ends, with no neighbors closer than a block.

This 10-room brick Italianate mansion was the last home in Galena of Captain Hezekiah Gear, who made his fortune by discovering one of area's largest lead mines. He came to Galena in 1827 and lived with his first wife in a log cabin. He was named "captain" during the Blackhawk War, and was thereafter known by that title. His children were raised in a different house near Gear and Bench streets.

In the 1840s, he served as a state senator. Stories from that time indicate he carried money in his hat and gave it freely to the needy, and he donated the land for construction of Grace Episcopal Church (it had been meeting in his home). Another story says that when Galena's town leaders turned down the railroad's request to build here, he told them, "Grass will grow in your streets."

Eventually, the house was inherited by nieces of his third wife. By the late 1960s, the home had deteriorated to a shell and was inhabited by transients and bats. Dr. Bob Brewer, a Galena dentist, bought it and put in many years of restoration.

Alyce Green bought the home and opened her B&B in August 1989, after retiring as a pharmacy technician from a Chicago-area hospital. She had stayed in B&Bs in Ireland, and found innkeeping appealing.

She found the house by accident. Alyce, her daughter and her son-in-law made a spontaneous day-trip to Galena. Her son-in-law, who is in real estate, started looking in the real estate windows in town. They were able to tour this house. "I got in the front door and about to the living room and said, 'This is it,' " she said. The downstairs ceilings are 14 feet high, upstairs they are 11 feet.

Guests may use the small parlor/smoking room, large double parlor with piano, kitchen, half-bath downstairs and patio outdoors.

Rooms and Rates: Three - All upstairs. Mary's Room has twin wrought iron beds, white spreads, birdseye maple furniture, pine plank floor, bath with tub/shower - $65. Clarissa's Room has queen walnut carved bed, red and white wallpaper, double whirlpool with hand-held shower - $85. Hamilton's Room has a double maple bed, brick outer walls, done in white and blue, bath with tub/shower - $65. Rates are double; single, $10 less. Add tax.

Meals: Continental breakfast is served in the kitchen or dining room at a time arranged the night before. It may include fresh fruit, homemade pear bread and/or pistachio coffeecake.

Dates Open: Year 'round

Smoking: First floor only (owner does)

Children: No

Pets: No

Handicapped Access: No

A/C: Central

Other/Group Uses: No

Location: From Highway 20, turn south at stoplight onto Bench Street, proceed straight on one-lane road up hill, then down gravel road. Main Street, 5 blocks.

Deposit: First night's lodging

Payment: Cash, personal or traveler's checks only

Colonial Guest House

1004 Park Ave.   Owner/Operator:
Galena, IL 61036   Mary C. Keller
815-777-0336

If you want quaint "country" decor, don't knock on Mary Keller's door. "Those horse collars and crocks and stuff. That stuff's from basements, woodsheds and barns. I like the finer things in life." So Mary's quarters practically are stuffed with Victorian furniture from the 1830s, cranberry glass, crystal chandeliers, marble statues and fireplaces, cut glass goblets and other art glass. "It shocks me, people don't know what a bone dish is, a butter dish is, what certain silverware is for."

Mary was "raised proper," along with five sisters, in a house on Bench Street. Her father was in the oil business in Tulsa. The family bought a farm here, but they lived in town Monday through Friday. The girls learned, among other things, how to set a proper table and how to dress like ladies.

But she's no pushover; some describe her as "very direct" or "candid." For instance, she feels some dilapidated buildings are not worth restoring. She also has strong opinions on B&Bs and shares them freely; she's been running her guest house since 1959, longer than anyone else in town. (The home had apartments but she had no desire to continue to be a landlady.) In the late '60s, she was known to turn away "people who came to the door with long hair and blue jeans. We didn't have people around here with long hair and blue jeans."

Her home was built in 1846 by Darius Hunkins, prominent contrator and railroad-builder. "My sister bought it in 1939 for $1,000 and I bought it in 1946 for $8,000," she said. For about 30 years, she's run an antique shop selling art glass on the first floor (she clearly feels that there's a big difference between *real* antiques that are valuable and country primitives). An elderly friend lives across the hall. Guest rooms are available on all three floors (Mary lives on the second), but that may change with redecorating. Guests may use the two back screened porches.

Rooms and Rates: Five units, including two apartments - All with private baths, color cable TV, antiques and some modern furniture. Mary noted she's planning on doing the rooms over; these are examples at the time of publication: Apt. A, private entrance on first floor from the back, small table and kitchenette, bath with older-style metal shower stall, modern sofa, double antique bed, green, blue and beige floral striped wallpaper. Room B is on second floor, private entrance, two twin antique beds with chenille spreads, red/orange antique settee, large print red floral wallpaper. $45 single, $55 double. Add tax.

Meals: Breakfast is set out on the porches or in the kitchen 8:30-9, "or guests can pick it up the night before." It may include rolls, cookies, Swiss Colony treats and fruit.

Dates Open: Year 'round

Children: Yes

Handicapped Access: No

Other/Group Uses: No

Smoking: "I don't dig it too much"

Pets: "Small ones"

A/C: "They don't need it;" ceiling fans

Location: Located in East Galena, facing the river. From Highway 20, turn south on Park Avenue. Main Street, 2 blocks.

Deposit: "Send a deposit — that's all."

Payment: Cash, personal or traveler's checks only

Comfort Guest House

1000 Third St.
Galena, IL 61036
815-777-3062

Owners/Operators:
Connie and Tom Sola

When Connie and Tom Sola came out to see Galena on a weekend jaunt from Chicago, they could not have known the changes in their lives this trip would precipitate. Six months later, in May 1984, they married at the Galena courthouse. A day later, they put an offer down on this house. Four months later, they opened three guest rooms in their B&B.

"We *really did* like Galena. We wanted a big house and Tom wanted a big porch," explained Connie. "We decided we would fill it up with guests."

Solas both gave up professional jobs in the Chicago area. Tom, a special education teacher and coach, got a job in Dubuque. Connie, an art major and master gardener, operates the B&B on weekends and sells advertising weekdays.

The brick house on a huge double lot was built in 1856 by William Snyder, a bank official and the founder of the Galena Insurance Company, which insured steamboats. Somehow his connections with steamboat owners resulted in the two marble fireplaces, made from imported marble and shipped to town.

Snyders had three children, and one of the daughters lived here until her death on June 22, 1947. "I don't know if you believe in coincidences," Connie said, "but I was born on June 23, 1947." Solas are only the fourth owners. The house was used as a church for a short period of time, then as private residences.

Solas left original walls, woodwork and some fixtures, but sanded floors, wallpapered, painted and carpeted. They put in raised bed gardens, where Connie grows flowers for the rooms, fruits and vegetables. Guests often enjoy the strawberries, melons and rhubarb in breakfast recipes (and many a seed or gardening tip has been swapped, as well). Breakfast is served on Grandma's silver in the dining room, where guests also may help themselves anytime to tea, hot chocolate, lemonade or iced tea, depending on the season. Guests are welcome to enjoy the fireplace or TV in the living room.

Rooms and Rates: Three - All upstairs with double beds and Connie's quilts; share two baths, one downstairs with tub/shower, one upstairs with original clawfoot tub, pull-chain toilet and marble sink. Champagne Room has bay window, white miniature print wallpaper, white iron bed. Ale Room has brass bed, pale yellow walls, navy carpet, adjoining room with twin bed. Wine Room has burgundy walls, wood floor, walnut bed. $65. Rate is single or double. Add tax.

Meals: Continental breakfast is served in the dining room at 8:30. It may include cold cereal, granola, fresh seasonal fruit, and homemade muffins or breads.

Dates Open: Weekends year 'round   **Smoking:** Living room only

Children: No   **Pets:** No

Handicapped Access: No   **A/C:** Window

Other/Group Uses: Family reunions, quilting clubs, ski groups.

Location: Located in East Galena, on the south corner of Highway 20 and Third Street. Main Street, 4 blocks.

Deposit: Confirmation by credit card

Payment: Cash, personal or traveler's checks, VISA or MasterCard

Craig Cottage

505 Dewey Ave.
Galena, IL 61036
815-777-1461
815-777-0482

Owners/Operators:
Galena Heritage, Inc.
(Kathy and Charlie Marsden,
Mark VanOsdol)

Captain Nathan Boone Craig, who married Daniel Boone's granddaughter in Kentucky, built this cottage above the Galena River in 1827. He was a captain of volunteers in the Blackhawk War of 1832. With thick stone blocks, Craig built the cottage into the hillside, supposedly to protect himself from Indian attack.

Indians originally settled this part of town, known as Old Town, because of natural springs. Craig's small cottage is believed to be one of the oldest homes in Galena. For 10 years, it consisted solely of one room with a fireplace. The upstairs was added about 1837. It was a single family residence until the early 1900s.

"Charlie grew up across the street," Innkeeper Kathy Marsden said of her husband. "He says it deteriorated to the point that it was a chicken coop." Pictures in an album show the sad state it was in before it was carefully rebuilt in the '60s by a local tavern owner, Race Kraehmer. It most recently was owned by a retired couple from Chicago who played up the "country" decor and had the house featured in an early Country Living magazine. The fieldstone fireplace with a Christmas tree was photographed for a Christmas card by Hallmark.

Marsdens and their partner Mark VanOsdol, an administrator for Clarke College in Dubuque, decided to purchase the building and operate it as a private guest house. They had little redecorating or furnishing to do. Kathy, an X-ray technician, and Charlie, a mechanical engineer in Dubuque, live right across the street and check guests in or help in other ways.

Upstairs is one small bedroom and the bathroom, plus a living room with a phone for guests' use. Downstairs is the other living room and kitchen with thick stone walls exposed. A fieldstone fireplace downstairs is supplied with firewood. The kitchen has a small microwave and other full-size appliances, plus utensils, staples, spices and leftover pancakes mixes and other items that former guests generously left behind. A washer/dryer is tucked away in a small utility room. The three-season porch overlooking the river has a small organ. A charcoal grill is out in back on a brick deck, above the wooded river valley.

Rooms and Rates: One bedroom upstairs, double brass bed. Sofa sleeper downstairs. Bathroom upstairs with tub/shower. $85 single or double, $100 family, $115 two couples. Midweek and multiple night discounts. Add tax.

Meals: Cook-your-own in a complete kitchen. Coffee, tea and other staples provided.

Dates Open: Year 'round   **Smoking:** Yes

Children: Yes   **Pets:** "Most pets with prior approval"

Handicapped Access: No   **A/C:** Window units upstairs

Other/Group Uses: No

Location: Follow Main Street north (it turns into Dewey). Cottage is on the right. Main Street shopping, 3 blocks.

Deposit: First night's lodging or confirmation by credit card

Payment: Cash, personal or traveler's checks, VISA or MasterCard

DeSoto House Hotel

230 S. Main St.
Galena, IL 61036
815-777-0090
1-800-343-6562

Owners/Operators:
Galena Associates, Inc.
(three Chicago men)
General Manager: George S. Bush

When the DeSoto House was re-opened in April 1986 after a massive $8 million renovation, a headline in the local paper noted, "History marches through the DeSoto House." That's close to literal truth. Parades and 25,000 people gathered to welcome home Galena resident General Ulysses S. Grant from the Civil War in 1865. Abraham Lincoln spoke against slavery from the DeSoto balcony in 1856, and Stephen Douglas spoke there two years later, and Teddy Roosevelt slept here. The DeSoto House also hosted Mark Twain, Susan B. Anthony, Horace Greeley and Ralph Waldo Emerson.

Opened in prosperous Galena in 1855, the $85,000 hotel was heralded as "the best hotel west of New York City." The five-story hotel was the epitome of elegance in that era.

The hotel survived a 1859 fire and the 1880 removal of her two top stories, but barely weathered the years when economic depression gripped Galena. Structurally unsound and posted as dangerous in 1978, the hotel stood empty for the first time while city officials and developers began feasibility studies and funding searches.

After restoration and new construction, in 1986 the hotel re-opened, but bankruptcy was declared. Then it opened and closed again. Now it has re-opened for the third time under new owners and managers.

Restaurants, a parking ramp, meeting and banquet rooms, cocktail lounges and a ballroom were part of the renovation. Shops and meeting rooms face an open courtyard, where lunch and dinner are served. Wood-work and masonry have been preserved wherever possible. Bellhops are present.

Rooms and Rates: 55 - Each with private bath, writing table, color cable TV and phone, decorated individually in period reproductions with country wallpapers. About half have a view of the Galena River and Grant Park. Four rooms have handicapped access. Rate range is $65 to $129 for a suite, double occupancy. Packages available. Off-season, midweek, multiple-night discounts. Add tax.

Meals: Breakfast is not included in the room rate. Three meals a day are available in hotel dining rooms or courtyard.

Dates Open: Year 'round

Smoking: Yes

Children: Yes (under 10 free)

Pets: No

Handicapped Access: Four rooms (elevator)

A/C: Central

Other/Group Uses: Meeting rooms, weddings, catering

Location: Hotel is on the east side of Main Street, about three blocks from floodgates.

Deposit: First night's lodging or confirmation with credit card

Payment: Cash, personal or traveler's checks, VISA, MasterCard or AMEX

DeZoya House B&B

1203 Third St.
Galena, IL 61036
815-777-1203

Owners/Operators:
Carol and Bill Preston

From the architecture and other "hints" hidden in the construction of this stone house, Innkeepers Carol and Bill Preston are led to believe that it was built in the early 1830s. The builder is believed to be David G. Bates, a financier, lead miner and owner of several steamboats. Bates, whose uncle, Moses Bates, founded Hannibal, Missouri, constructed this as a nine-bedroom home.

John Paul DeZoya, who often did business with Bates, bought the home from him in 1837. DeZoya, a Swiss immigrant who came to Galena in 1833, was the first county treasurer. He probably lived alone in this large house. The home stayed in DeZoya's family for years, then had a succession of other owners.

Prestons first bought the cottage next door as a summer home and retreat from Chicago, where Carol and Bill restored historic buildings and developed real estate. They spent more and more time in Galena and decided to live here.

The stone house came up for sale. "This building was going to ruin and there were birds flying in and out of the windows," Bill said. "We wanted to buy it and restore it. We didn't know what we'd do with it, but we wanted to do right by it." Operating a B&B helped justify living in Galena full-time. Besides, the couple had collected Federal antiques of the 1780-1820 period, perfect for the home.

Prestons bought the house in August 1987 and began major work, including a new roof, all major heating and cooling systems, re-plastering ceilings and adding bathrooms. "It needed lots of linoleum, accoustical tile and paneling removed," Bill said. Many original doors and fixtures were found and restored.

Prestons can give names, styles and origins of all antiques. They have a second floor suite and share the house with guests. Guests may use the second floor balcony, screened back porch and TV room and library.

Rooms and Rates: Four - All with queen beds, cypress floors with antique Persian rugs or carpet, private baths. Two rooms on second floor have carved, four-poster canopy beds, baths with shower only. Two rooms on third floor have dormered windows, baths with tub/shower. One has sleigh bed, done in blue; other has pine cannonball bed, done in pale green. $75 weekends, $70 weekdays. Rates are double; single, $5 less. No third persons in rooms. Multiple night discounts. Two-night minimum stay required some weekends; three-night minimum holiday weekends. Add tax.

Meals: Breakfast is served in the dining room at 9. It may include fruit breads or muffins, fresh fruit, grits, and quiche, ham and eggs, pancakes or eggs benedict.

Dates Open: Year 'round

Children: Over 12

Handicapped Access: No

Other/Group Uses: No

Smoking: Not in guest rooms

Pets: No

A/C: Central

Location: Located in East Galena at the south end of Third Street. From Highway 20, turn south on Third, go to the end. Main Street, 5 blocks.

Deposit: First night's lodging or confirmation by credit card

Payment: Cash, personal or traveler's checks, VISA, MasterCard or AMEX

The Eagles' Nest & Amber Creek Farm Cottage

410 S. High St. & off Tower Road
Galena, IL & Elizabeth, IL
c/o Amber Creek Farm, P.O. Box 5
Galena, IL 61036
815-598-3301

Owners/Operators:
Kate and Doug Freeman

Kate and Doug Freeman, who formerly operated a B&B in their Elizabeth farmhouse, now rent out two restored cottages to overnight guests.

One, named years ago as "the Eagles' Nest," is in Galena at 410 S. High St., near Central School (the old high school-turned-condo with the clock tower). It is a brick, two-story Federal style home. It is believed to have been built by J.W. Robinson in 1842 as rental property, and was located in one of Galena's black neighborhoods (the African Episcopal Methodist Church used to stand nearby. Robinson also was the builder of what turned out to be Grant's first Galena home.) There was no running water in the home until the 1940s, and no indoor plumbing until 1957. Kate bought the Eagles' Nest in 1975 and lived there until 1980.

The other rental unit (not pictured) is the Farm Cottage, the old summer kitchen and smokehouse next to the farmhouse, located about three miles outside Elizabeth. The kitchen was built detached from the farmhouse by the Wand family, two branches of whom owned and lived on the 300-acre farm until 1945, then sold it to the Freemans in 1985. Kate and Doug gutted the kitchen and put in a living area with a skylit loft bed and turned the small smokehouse into a bathroom. Later they added a kitchen area, another room with a fireplace, plus a whirlpool. Guests are free to enjoy the wildlife and hiking trails, x-c skiing and tobogganing.

For either accommodation, guests usually check in at the farm, 18 miles from Galena, or make special arrangements.

Rooms and Rates: Two private cottages. The Eagles' Nest cottage has antiques and country decor. Living/dining room has cast iron fireplace, full kitchen has antique gas/wood stove. One bedroom above kitchen has double bed, wood plank floors, floral wallpaper; other bedroom above living room has queen bed, sitting room with crib; bath with clawfoot tub/shower - $225 per couple for two nights. The Amber Creek Farm Cottage has kitchenette, fireplace in living room, queen bed, bath with double whirlpool/hand-held shower, short attic loft above bedroom - $245 per couple for two nights.
Each additional person, $10. Midweek discounts. Two-night minimum stay required weekends. Add tax.

Meals: Cook-your-own meals. Coffee and fresh baked goods, such as nut bread or lemon pound cake, are provided.

Dates open: Year 'round

Children: Yes

Handicapped Access: No

Other/Group Uses: No

Smoking: Yes

Pets: Yes - $15 extra

A/C: Window units

Location: The Eagles' Nest is near Central School; turn north on High Street from Highway 20. Directions given. Amber Creek Farm and cottage are located 18 miles from Galena, 3 miles from Elizabeth. Map sent.

Deposit: $75 or confirmation by credit card

Payment: Cash, personal or traveler's checks, VISA, MasterCard, AMEX or Discover

Farmers' Home Hotel

334 Spring St.
Galena, IL 61036
815-777-3456
1-800-373-3456
FAX 815-777-3470

Owner/Operator:
Bonnie and Tom Ogie-Kristianson
Innkeeper: Elissa Gunning

In the 1860s, when farmers came to market in Galena, they often could not make a return wagon trip in one day. The Farmers' Home Hotel, just a few blocks from downtown, "was a little step higher than a boarding house," said Tom Kristianson. Rooms were located over a store and bakery, built and run by the Vogel brothers, a busy place in Galena's heyday.

The Galena Gazette once reported that for nearly a century the Vogel name meant "honesty and fair deals," and one gets the sense that Tom tries to carry on the tradition. The restoration work has made the hotel modern while maintaining or authentically restoring as much as possible, including the original room numbers on doors and hand-graining in woodwork. "We're real purists," Tom said. "We don't equate bad restoration with bad taste, we equate it with immorality."

When Tom and a friend bought the hotel in January 1985, only a few downstairs rooms were being used. They acted as general contractors, used plenty of their own sweat equity, and saw that the floor plan stayed the same. The building needed to be rewired, replumbed, replastered, receilinged, wallpapered, carpeted, air conditioned and wired for cable TV, which is available by request. Seven rooms opened in May 1986.

Downstairs, the former store and bakery are a meeting room and a breakfast restaurant, open to the public. Anything on the menu is included in guests' room rate (tips not included). Homemade jams and breads, their own naturally-raised and locally-processed breakfast meats, and other general store items are for sale.

Tom installed an outdoor hot tub on the hillside. The Spring Street Tavern has been built on the side. A fax machine is available for guests' use.

Rooms and Rates: Nine rooms, two suites - All with private baths with tubs and phones, double or queen antique brass and wood beds, decorated with antiques, comforters and quilts, and country wallpaper, done in beiges, light purples and whites. Rooms - $85. Two-room suites - $115. Rates are double; single, $10 less. Each additional person, $10. Packages available. Off-season, midweek discounts. Two-night minimum stay required weekends. Add tax.

Meals: Breakfast is served downstairs in the restaurant or delivered to the guest room, included in room rate. Menu includes award-winning local bacon, Hobo Hash (potatoes, onions, bacon or ham, broccoli and cheese, covered with cheddar and sour cream), omelettes, eggs, fruit pancakes and fresh-squeezed orange juice.

Dates Open: Year 'round   **Smoking:** In three smoking rooms only

Children: Over 10   **Pets:** No

Handicapped Access: No   **A/C:** Central

Other/Group Uses: Meeting and dining facilities on premises. Together, the "Spring Street Corridor" inns (also including Renaissance Vintage Suites, Mother's Country Inn and Spring Street Guest House) can host bus tours.

Location: On the west/south side of Highway 20, 2 blocks from Main Street.

Deposit: First night's lodging or confirmation by credit card

Payment: Cash, personal or traveler's checks, VISA, MasterCard, AMEX, Discover, Diners Club or Carte Blanche

Farster's Executive Inn

305 N. Main St.
Galena, IL 61036
815-777-9125
1-800-545-8551

Owners/Operators:
Sandra and Bob Farster

Movie actress Joanna Cassidy stayed here one weekend after filming a movie in Chicago. She ended up having her picture taken with Farster's kids, and inviting Bob and Sandy to the "wrap" party after filming was completed.

From the street, if the building looks like a general store, it's no wonder. It was built as such about 1845. Since 1900, it operated as Alexander Grocery, Genz Grocery, Herrick's Grocery and Market, Metzger's Grocery, and Sprecht and Alexander. In 1970, it was Oster's Restaurant.

When Robert Farster, Jr., bought it on a whim in 1985, it had been a pool hall. He and Sandy had ideas of opening an antique shop. "But neither of us could turn loose of antiques. If I went to an auction, I couldn't turn around and sell it," Sandy said. Instead, Bob masterminded a guest facility. He and other workers rebuilt the interior above, behind and below the former grocery, now the lobby.

Farsters come to Galena on weekends from their Dixon, Ill., home, or have an innkeeper. They have a 1929 Buick, a '38 Plymouth and an old-fashioned "bus" in which Bob offers tours of town and countryside and, sometimes, weddings.

All guests may use the deck in back, the pool table in the renovated basement, and the eight-person hot tub in a redwood/cedar hot tub room also in the basement, with fresh towels stacked there.

Rooms and Rates: Four apartments, two rooms - All have "country" or Victorian wallpaper and antiques or folk art. Suite 1 is the old storage area, now a large sitting area with exposed brick walls, TV, sofa sleeper, recliner. Modern kitchen with deck, bedroom with double bed and skylight, bath with tub/shower - $95 double, $110 for four. Suite 2 has living area with sofa sleeper, recliner, TV, microwave, small fridge; one bedroom with double bed; bath with tub/shower - $90, $100 for four. Rooms 3 and 4 have one double bed each, TV, small fridge and bath with shower only - $65. Suite 5 has two bedrooms, large living area between bedrooms with TV and small fridge - $100 double, $120 for four. Suite 6 has huge living area with sleeper sofa, TV, dining room, large separate kitchen with pine floor, screened deck with gas grill; two bedrooms each with double bed, one with original skylight tower; bath with tub/shower - $110 double, $125 four, $140 six. Midweek, weekly rental discounts. Add tax.

Meals: Continental breakfast is available in the lobby 7:30 to 11. It includes donuts and sweet rolls.

Dates Open: Year 'round   **Smoking:** Yes

Children: Yes   **Pets:** Small pets OK

Handicapped Access: Suite 1 has street level access, two steps

A/C: Window units in Suites 5 and 6, central in rest of building

Other/Group Uses: Weddings in classic cars or bus

Location: On North Main Street

Deposit: Confirmation by credit card

Payment: Cash, personal or traveler's checks, VISA, MasterCard or Discover

Felt Manor Guest House

125 S. Prospect St.
Galena, IL 61036
815-777-9093
1-800-383-2830

Owners/Operators:
Sandra and Harry Hemlock

As the owner of a dry goods store and director of a bank, Lucius Felt was, indeed, well-to-do. His hilltop mansion had 24 rooms and more than 7,000 square feet. It was Greek Revival style, but in 1874 the Felts had a mansard roof added, making it Second Empire. The home also is known for "Felt's Folly," 74 steps chiseled into the hill in the 1860s at a cost of $40,000.

From 1939 to 1977, it was owned by Gladys and Ado Genz, department store owners. In 1986, it was purchased by Harry and Sandra Hemlock.

"We bought it for our own home. It is our home first and a B&B second," Harry explained. Hemlocks operate a business making decorative Victorian fans and other products. They clearly had more space than they needed and decided to re-open the former B&B to guests.

"We are old house preservationists, and you get caught up in it," said Sandra. This is their fourth home restoration. Outside, the original porches and walks are being rebuilt using historic photos for guides, and the exterior is being painted in four colors. Inside, the house was rewired, replumbed and the chimneys were rebuilt and relined. Rooms were wallpapered and decorated authentic to the period.

Hemlocks have a third floor suite and share the house with guests. Guests may use the first two floors, including the front parlor with fireplace, and the music room with two grand pianos and a pump organ, the library and the dining room. Hemlocks stress there is no smoking anywhere on the property, indoors or outside.

Rooms and Rates: Five - All upstairs, all with original sinks in room and double antique beds. Katherine's Room has carved bed, cherub lamp fixtures, done in pink, white and grey, private bath with shower only - $75. Other four rooms share bath at end of hall with tub/shower. Another bath will be available in 1991 on first floor. Gladys' Room has blue and white floral wallpaper, white iron bed and twin bed, view of downtown - $65. Lucius Felt Room has bold Victorian wallpaper in black, gold and burgundy, view of town - $65. Margaret's Room has white iron bed, white furniture, done in rose, beige and white - $60. Aunt Martha's Room has high carved headboard, currently done in peach - $60. Rates are single or double. Each additional person, $10. Off-season, midweek, multiple night discounts. Two-night minimum stay required some weekends. Add tax.

Meals: Continental breakfast is served in the dining room "at 8 sharp." It may include fruit, muffins, homemade breads or cinnamon rolls, all made with organic ingredients and whole-grain flours.

Dates Open: Year 'round

Smoking: Neither indoors nor outdoors

Children: Over 14

Pets: No

Handicapped Access: No

A/C: Window units

Other/Group Uses: Weddings up to 30 with catering arranged. Dining room seats 16.

Location: House faces Prospect Street on the hill, but entrance and parking is off High Street from the back.

Deposit: First night's lodging or confirmation by credit card

Payment: Cash, personal or traveler's checks, VISA, MasterCard or AMEX

Grandview Guest Home

113 S. Prospect St.
Galena, IL 61036
815-777-1387
1-800-373-0732

Owners/Operators:
Marjie and Harry Dugan

It's hard to argue with the name of this B&B. D.H. Lamberson, a Galena photographer and sewing machine dealer, knew a good thing when he saw it, and he built his home on this hilltop site in 1870. From the front porch swing, there's a clear view of nearly all of East Galena, Grant Park and much of downtown below.

Lamberson owned the home only until 1875, when he sold it for $2,800 to Henry Wallace. Wallace owned a clothing shop, and one that bore his name operated at 109 S. Main St. in the early 1900s.

In 1986, Marjie and Harry Dugan became the seventh owners. As newlyweds who had been to Galena for getaways, they moved here from a Chicago suburb. Harry retired from banking and now sells real estate in town, and Marjie left her GMC truck business. Their neighbors two doors down, Sandra and Harry Hemlock at Felt Manor, talked them into opening a B&B. "They said, 'What are you two doing over here rattling around in this big house by yourselves?' " Harry said.

Dugans keep a first-floor parlor, which had been added in 1890, for themselves and have a second-floor bedroom. The rest of the house is open to guests. On the first floor, the dining room has elaborate carved oak woodwork and leaded glass. Two parlors have a TV, woodstove and grand piano for guests' use.

Relatively little needed to be done to turn the home into a B&B. "We were very fortunate," Marjie said. Nearly the entire house was rewallpapered in subtle florals and other "country" patterns, and some electrical and plumbing work was completed. Family heirlooms and antiques were used to furnish it.

Rooms and Rates: Three - All upstairs. Blue Room has a double sleigh bed and twin wood bed, done in blue floral wallpaper, with pine plank floors and an oriental rug - $55. Pink Room has a queen wood bed and twin sleigh bed, lace curtains, pine plank floors and burgundy oriental rug - $55. Rose Room, in the former servants' quarters, has a double bed with lacy comforter, done in rose and cream. It may be rented with a sitting room and private bath with shower only next door - $70. If so, other two rooms share a bath in hall with clawfoot tub/shower. If not, all three rooms may share the bath with shower only - $55 each. Rates are double or single. Seniors, $5 less. Child under 12, $10. Two-night minimum stay required some weekends. Add tax.

Meals: Breakfast is served in the dining room 8:30-9 and includes muffins, nut bread, bar cookies and quiche or French toast.

Dates Open: Year 'round

Smoking: In parlors only

Children: Yes

Pets: No

Handicapped Access: No

A/C: Window units

Other/Group Uses: Garden weddings up to 50, catering arranged; small meetings up to 15.

Location: The house is off the side street Washington, which turns into a staircase that runs down the hill to Prospect. Come up High Street, turn onto Washington to park at the side of the house.

Deposit: Half of room rate or confirmation by credit card

Payment: Cash, personal or traveler's checks, VISA, MasterCard, AMEX or Discover

Harris House B&B

713 S. Bench St.
Galena, IL 61036
815-777-1611

Owners/Operators:
Carol and Bert Carney

Robert Scribe Harris is said to have been the quiet one of the Harris brothers. He often bailed his brother Daniel out of trouble. But both boys were hard-working and smart. As teens, they secured their future by founding and operating a lead mine. They defended their claim and they held onto their profits, enabling them in 1833 to build the first steamboat north of St. Louis. Robert was also a successful engineer. Daniel built his house a block up the hill on South Prospect, known as the Steamboat House.

Robert built this home in 1836 in a style showing French influence. The lower floor below the Prospect Street level was once the root cellar, stable and kitchen. The guest cottage in the back, remodeled by previous owners, was once a pigeon or chicken coop.

The house has 52 leaded glass windows that were added in the 1920s, constructed by a partner of Frank Lloyd Wright who also designed the Board of Education building in Chicago. Those who look closely will see the "H" for "Harris" in the center of the windows.

Carol and Bert Carney bought the operating B&B and reopened it in 1987 after removing shag carpet, adding stenciling and making utility improvements.

Guests may use the front porch swing, sun porch, library and TV or parlor with fireplace.

Rooms and Rates: Three rooms in main house - All upstairs with handmade quilts on queen pencil post beds, twin beds, ceiling fans, wood floor with rag rugs. Robert Harris Room has navy and white Victorian wallpaper, window seat, skylit bath with tub/shower - $75. Daniel Harris Room has blue and white decor, shares bath with River Room - $65. River Room has yellow and peach decor; shared art deco bath has tub/shower - $65.
One guest cottage - Scribe's Cottage has small living room with small fridge, color cable TV, modern sofa; small bedroom has double iron bed with quilt, bath with shower only, done in blue and white country wallpaper, candystriped carpet, window A/C - $80.
Rates are weekend; weekdays, $5 less. Cash payment, $5 less. Rates are double; single, $5 less. Each additional adult, $20. Two-night minimum stay required weekends. Add tax.

Meals: Breakfast is served in the dining room at 8:30 with blueberry, pumpkin or bran muffins. At 9, breakfast may include fresh fruit, quiche or pancakes, bacon or sausage.

Dates Open: Year 'round

Smoking: No

Children: No

Pets: No (cats on first floor)

Handicapped Access: No

A/C: Central (window in cottage)

Other/Group Uses: No

Location: From Highway 20, turn south on Bench 1 block. Main Street, 2 blocks.

Deposit: First night's lodging or confirmation by credit card

Payment: Cash, personal or traveler's checks, VISA, MasterCard or AMEX

Hellman Guest House

318 Hill St.
Galena, IL 61036
815-777-3638

Owner/Operator:
 Merilyn Tommaro
Innkeeper: Rachel Stilson

This Queen Anne Victorian, built of Galena brick in 1895 by John V. Hellman, was home to the prominent Galena merchant, Wenona, his wife, and their three daughters, after whom guest rooms are named. The home reflected the wealth of Hellman, his father, a retail grocer, and Wenona's father, a steamboat captain.

The hilltop home also was owned by Congressman Leo Allen, who was able to pass legislation to construct downtown Galena's levee.

Merilyn Tommaro was not in the market for a home in Galena when she and a friend came to town at Thanksgiving 1986 for a getaway from Chicago. "I had been thinking of moving back to Duluth — I grew up there." She'd move after her sons were out of school and then she could attend to drawing and selling her art, perhaps acting as a landlord in a duplex.

"We needed a room for the night and we stayed here and it was for sale. I just sort of went ga-ga over the thing," she recalls. Thinking eventually she'd move here to do art in the attic, she bought the house, which was operating as a B&B, and opened July 3, 1987. She's added private baths and central air, stripped woodwork and wallpapered in a light "modern Victorian" decor. She also installed an apartment for Rachel Stilson, who is full-time innkeeper; Merilyn commutes on weekends. Rachel grew up in Galena and has had years of innkeeping experience; she used to work at the Historical Museum and can answer many guests' questions.

Decor is in antiques and reproductions, with original woodwork and stained glass windows. Guests have use of the parlor and dining rooms, and the telescope pointed across the river for viewing architecture. The front porch is being rebuilt for guests' enjoyment.

Rooms and Rates: Four - All upstairs with private baths. The Hellman (master bedroom) in tower alcove has view of town, queen brass bed, done in deep green, rose and white, bath with inlaid tile and shower only - $89. The Pauline has white floral print wallpaper, queen white iron and brass bed, original sink in corner, bath with shower only - $69. The Irene has double carved oak bed, done in blue and white, bath with shower only - $69. The Eleanor has double quasi-four-poster bed, carpeted, done in rose and white, bath with inlaid tile and claw foot tub/shower - $69. Rates are double; single, $5 less. Off-season and midweek discounts. Two-night minimum stay required weekends. Add tax.

Meals: Continental breakfast is served in the dining room 8:30-9:30. It may include fresh fruit, homebaked muffins, nut breads and coffeecake.

Dates Open: Year 'round

Smoking: In library only

Children: Over 12

Pets: No

Handicapped Access: No

A/C: Central

Other/Group Uses: Small weddings up to 20

Location: From Highway 20, turn north on High Street. B&B is on the corner of Hill and High Streets; park in back and come around to the front door. Main Street, 2 blocks up the hill (one block is stairs).

Deposit: First night's lodging or confirmation by credit card

Payment: Cash, personal or traveler's checks, VISA, MasterCard or AMEX

Mother's Country Inn
349 Spring St.
Galena, IL 61036
815-777-3153

Owner/Operator:
Patricia Laury

Built in 1838 as a "double house," this Federalist Townhouse was used as a duplex for 144 years, until Pat Laury bought it. Perhaps the longest it was owned by one family was from 1905 until the mid-1950s, when the Johnson family lived in one side, raised 10 children there, and rented out the other side.

Pat has transformed the identical twin units into guest rooms upstairs, a guest room and sitting area in half of the downstairs, and her quarters on the other side downstairs. She found the building in need of major restoration, bought it, started work in 1982, and opened guest rooms in 1983.

"I had traveled in B&Bs in Europe and California and in inns in the South," she said. "I spent a summer before I bought this place out in California and I drove up Highway 101 and stayed in B&Bs in Eureka and Mendocino. It was 'the in thing' there and I knew it was coming this way."

Restoration involved gutting the interior and raising the center of the building a foot "and, of course, it's still not level! I just went right down to the studs and started over," trying not to change the layout or structure.

Guests have a private entrance and a downstairs sitting room, which has a TV, gas fireplace and antiques, most of which are for sale.

About six months after buying the brick house, she bought "The Little Blue House" next door, believed to be one of the oldest frame houses in Galena, built about 1830. The architecture shows French influence. It was built of cypress.

Pat plans to open four suites in another adjacent building in 1990.

Rooms and Rates: Seven - All with antique beds that have been enlarged. First floor room has queen brass bed with brocade spread, floral print wallpaper, private bath with shower only - $65. Upstairs, all six rooms have a sink in the room, share two baths with tub/shower - $55 each. Examples include: #1 queen brass bed, hand-crocheted spread, wicker furniture, blue and white wallpaper. #3 has two twin carved oak Rockford beds made in Rockford, Ill., mini-print wallpaper in peach. Rates are double; single, $10 less. Off-season and midweek discounts. Two-night minimum stay required weekends for long-term reservations. Add tax. The Little Blue House is rented to one party, sleeps six in two bedrooms plus sofa sleeper, full kitchen, bath with shower only - $200 for one couple, $25 each additional couple, for three weekend nights or four weeknights. Add tax.

Meals: Continental breakfast is served in the sitting room or on the screened porch beginning at 8:30. It may include rolls or muffins.

Dates Open: Year 'round

Smoking: Some guest rooms

Children: Yes

Pets: No ("My dog won't let me")

Handicapped Access: No

A/C: Central

Other/Group Uses: Can provide accommodations for 20 in main inn. Together, the "Spring Street Corridor" inns (also including Renaissance Vintage Suites, Farmer's Home Hotel and Spring Street Guest House) can host bus tours; meeting and dining facilities at Farmer's Home Hotel.

Location: On the corner of Highway 20 and High Street. Main Street, 3 blocks.

Deposit: Confirmation by credit card

Payment: Cash, personal or traveler's checks, VISA or MasterCard

Park Avenue Guest House

208 Park Ave.
Galena, IL 61036
815-777-1075

Owners/Operators:
Sharon and John Fallbacher

Sharon and John Fallbacher worked in Chicago and already were restoring their Galena miner's 1852 cottage when this grand Queen Anne came on the market in 1988. They saw it on a Sunday, made a down payment the next Saturday, sold their suburban Chicago home the next Saturday, and had moved in within two months.

Fallbachers fell hard for this huge 1893 home. It was constructed by J.B. Ginn, who became mayor of Galena, for Bias Sampson. Sampson graduated from Annapolis in 1881 and is believed to have been aboard the USS Maine ("Remember the Maine!") battleship prior to the Spanish-American War.

The Sampson family retained ownership until 1968, but had converted the home to apartments. "Half the people in Galena had lived there," Sharon said. Fallbachers are the fifth owners after Sampsons.

Though conversion to a private residence already was underway, Fallbachers had their work cut out for them. Much of that fell to Sharon, who worked seven days a week on the house. They added three bathrooms, refinished 17 doors, and hung 190 rolls of wallpaper. Except for plumbing and wiring, they did the work themselves, completely redecorating, buying a houseful of furniture and refinishing much of it. The dining room alone involved removing paneling, then two layers of wallpaper, then a layer of paint, then more wallpaper. All that was accomplished in seven months, in time to open on Memorial Day 1989.

Guests can use the hammock under the maples, the iron elevator door gazebo, the parlors and the VCR. It's not unusual for summer or fall guests and innkeepers to order a pizza and enjoy it on the screened wrap-around porch. The porch is lighted with kerosene lamps and has wrought iron rockers.

Rooms and Rates: Three - All upstairs with antiques, a ceiling fan, antique beds adapted to queen-size, working transoms above the doors, and private baths with showers only. Anna Suite has a sitting room in turret with daybed, pedestal sink in room, done in pink with pink, black and green wallpaper above chair rail - $95. Miriam Room has grey iron bed with yellow spread, rose chaise lounge, antique rocker - $65. Lucille Room is done in grey and mauve with grey iron bed - $65. Rates are single or double. Off-season, midweek, senior and multiple-night discounts. Two-night minimum stay required some weekends. Add tax.

Meals: Continental breakfast is served at the kitchen table or on the screened porch at a time arranged the night before. It may include cold cereals, fresh seasonal fruit and homemade bread or muffins.

Dates Open: Year 'round

Children: Over 12

Handicapped Access: No

Other/Group Uses: No

Smoking: In public rooms only (owners do)

Pets: No (elderly dog on premises)

A/C: Central

Location: Located in East Galena near the end of Park Avenue. Main Street, 2 blocks if Meeker Street Foot Bridge is open, 6 blocks via Grant Park Foot Bridge.

Deposit: First night's lodging or confirmation by credit card

Payment: Cash, personal or traveler's checks, VISA, MasterCard or AMEX

Queen Anne Guest House

200 Park Ave.
Galena, IL 61036
815-777-3849

Owners/Operators:
Kathleen Martin and
Cary Mandelka

Kathleen Martin and Cary Mandelka came to Galena from Chicago for their honeymoon in 1985. They stayed in a couple B&Bs, and before they went back to Chicago, they had decided they wanted to have a B&B of their own. "But we thought we'd have one on the East Coast," Kathleen said.

For the next two years, "everytime we'd sit in a traffic jam, we'd say, 'We're going to go live in Galena where there's only one traffic light,' " she said. In January 1987 they bought this house, an ornate 1891 corner home.

It's no wonder that there are a thousand knobs, turrets, overhangs and other gingerbread and fretwork outside. The home was built for William Ridd, who made and sold windows, sashes and doors. He and Louisa, his wife, raised a family here.

A doctor once had an office here, and the grand home was eventually converted into apartments. When Kathleen and Cary moved in, more than two decades of "being let go" had to be attended to.

Doing the work themselves, "we had illusions of finishing it in one year," Cary said. Downstairs, woodwork and floors were sanded, stained and varnished. The stairway had been painted blue and carpeted, which had to be redone. Private baths were installed. Wallpaper was stripped, walls replastered and new paper hung.

Outside, it took four months to get the shingle siding off, fill in the nail holes and fix up the clapboard. Painters estimated $15,000, so Kathy and Cary painted themselves. Each fell through rotted porches, which were then rebuilt.

The B&B opened in September 1989. Guests have use of the entire downstairs, including a library, parlor and living room with VCR. Coffee and cookies, baked in the 1920s Magic Chef gas range, are always available.

Rooms and Rates: Three - All upstairs with ceiling fans, electric blankets and private baths. Room 1 has double antique bed with antique quilt, blue carpet and beige/blue mini-print wallpaper, large bathroom with clawfoot tub/hand-held shower. Room 2 is a corner room, queen brass bed, mauve carpet and mini-print wallpaper with white accents, bath has clawfoot tub/hand-held shower. Room 3 has white iron double bed, done in forest green carpet and mini-print wallpaper with white accents, bath down hall with clawfoot tub/shower. $60 weekends, $50 weekdays. Rates are single or double. Senior, off-season, multiple night discounts available. Add tax.

Meals: Continental breakfast is served in the dining room when guests come down. It may include home-baked bran and another kind of muffins, coffeecake or rolls, fresh seasonal fruit salad and hard-boiled eggs.

Dates Open: Year 'round   **Smoking:** No

Children: By special arrangement   **Pets:** No (sweet dog on premises)

Handicapped Access: No   **A/C:** Window units

Other/Group Uses: Small weddings, retreats and seminars up to 20

Location: Located in East Galena at the end of Park Avenue at the corner of Meeker. Main Street, 2 blocks if Meeker Street Foot Bridge is open, 6 blocks via Grant Park Foot Bridge.

Deposit: First night's lodging or confirmation by credit card

Payment: Cash, personal or traveler's checks, VISA or MasterCard

Renaissance Vintage Suites and Rooms

324 Spring St. and 117 N. Main St.
P.O. Box 291   Owners/Operators:
Galena, IL 61036   Victoria and Terry Cole
815-777-0123

If, a dozen years ago, anyone had told Terry Cole that in 1990 he would be renovating run-down buildings, renting suites to overnight guests and serving as mayor of Galena, he wouldn't have believed them.

Cole was painting houses at the time. But they often needed masonry and carpentry repairs, so he would subcontract it. "Then, for something to do in the winter, I ended up buying a house." He and Vickie, an interior decorator, restored their Federal-style house on Bench Street. Almost before he knew it, he had more and more people working for him, and he was investing in some buildings himself.

The main inn is in the Beltram Building, circa 1857, formerly Mellers Saloon for the Fulton Brewery, which is right behind it. Downstairs, Vickie has a studio and a paint and wallpaper supply store; she decorates all the suites and rooms. On the second floor is a two-bedroom guest suite. The third floor is three guest rooms. Next door is another building that will offer four suites in summer 1990 (all guests will check in with an innkeeper here). Down on Main Street, in another building Coles own, is one guest apartment.

Meanwhile, Terry was elected mayor and spends some time in the Mayor's Office at City Hall. "I'm renovating that, too. When I went in there was plaster falling off the ceiling and plastic curtains on the windows." Not for long.

Rooms and Rates: All decorated in antiques, country French or Early American wallpaper, color cable TV, phone, private baths, central air, kitchen access.
Beltram Building - one suite; three rooms. Suite on second floor sleeps six adults in two bedrooms, living room with sofa sleeper; full modern kitchen, leaded glass accents; bath with tub/shower - $100 double, $20 for each additional couple.
Upstairs, three rooms share kitchen. Example includes #1 with canopy queen bed, done in burgundy, bath with tub/shower across hall - $75 double.
Building next door - four suites. Some with fireplaces, whirlpool tubs, loft bedroom; hot tub installed in root cellar under hillside in back - $120 per couple.
Main Street apartment has one bedroom with queen four-poster bed, skylit kitchen, living room with sofa sleeper, view of Market House - $100 double, $120 two couples. Off-season and midweek discounts. Two-night minimum stay required peak-season weekends. Add tax.

Meals: Cook-your-own in complete kitchens with full-size microwaves, conventional ovens and stoves, refrigerators, coffee-maker, etc. Coffee is supplied.

Dates Open: Year 'round   **Smoking:** Yes

Children: "Welcome" (playpen available)   **Pets:** "Small pets in suites only"

Handicapped Access: 1 suite   **A/C:** Central

Other/Group Uses: Together, the "Spring Street Corridor" inns (also including Farmer's Home Hotel, Mother's Country Inn and Spring Street Guest House) can host bus tours; meeting and dining facilities at Farmer's Home Hotel.

Location: On Highway 20 at corner of Prospect next to Fulton Brewery, 1 block from Main Street. (All guests check in here.)

Deposit: First night's lodging or confirmation by credit card

Payment: Cash, personal or traveler's checks, VISA, MasterCard or AMEX

Spring Street Guest House

414 Spring St.   Owners/Operators:
Galena, IL 61036   Sandra and Charles Fach
815-777-0354

This stone house, built in 1876 as an ice house for the City Brewery, is unusual enough. But an innkeeper always adds special touches, and when the innkeeper is a sculptor, painter and potter, the house reflects the artist.

In the Deluxe Suite, for instance, Charles Fach has installed a gas stove, surrounded by 3-D ceramic tiles he cast of 28 fish and animal (mostly dog) motifs. The bathroom, originally a root cellar and now a beautiful white-tiled enclave, has the longest continuous towel racks in the Tri-State area, built by Charles: 13.5-feet-long black steel rods, held in place in a bronze replica of Butch's head (Butch is the family dog. The former family dog's bronze head, in duplicate, is also on display.) Light fixtures are of bronze oak leaves. Even the drawings are Charles'.

The building itself was one of three in the City Brewery "complex." Rudolph Speier, who had worked in the Fulton Brewery just down the street, started City Brewery and made German Lager. "That was the first drive for 'light' beer," Charles said, placating some temperance advocates with its lower alcohol content. The times have gone full-cycle: now that super-light beers have taken taste out of beer, micro-breweries such as Speier's are making a comeback.

In order to brew the light stuff, a constant 45-degree temperature was needed, and demand and competition dictated summer brewing was necessary, so the ice house was built. Ice was cut from the Galena River and stored in sawdust layers here. But after refrigeration came in, the building was converted to residential use.

Charles and Sandra, a kindergarten teacher, bought this house and theirs next door in 1980, continuing to rent apartments. Then they converted the ice house to the Guest House in 1985. Their house, where guests eat breakfast, was once a tea room, and John Dillinger was said to have been served there.

Rooms and Rates: Two - Both suites have a sitting area with color TV, a king custom-made bed with step stool, and a private bath. Front Suite has bed with people figures on four bedposts, animals on bed "feet," done in black and gold Victorian wallpaper; bath has large shower only with handmade tiles - $59.95. Deluxe Suite is done in outdoor motif with pheasant wallpaper; bed posts have Diana the Huntress figures, root cellar bath has clawfoot tub and separate tiled shower - $79.95. Rates are single or double. Each additional person, $15. Two-night minimum stay required weekends. Add tax.

Meals: Breakfast is served in Fach's kitchen next door at 9. It may include French toast, omelettes or an egg casserole, sausage and muffins.

Dates Open: Year 'round

Smoking: No

Children: Over 8

Pets: No

Handicapped Access: No

A/C: Central

Other/Group Uses: Together, the "Spring Street Corridor" inns (also including Renaissance Vintage Suites, Farmer's Home Hotel and Mother's Country Inn) can host bus tours; meeting and dining facilities at Farmer's Home Hotel.

Location: On west side of Highway 20, four blocks from Main Street.

Deposit: Confirmation by credit card

Payment: Cash, personal or traveler's checks, VISA, MasterCard, AMEX, Discover, Diners Club or Carte Blanche

Stillman's Country Inn

513 Bouthillier St.
Galena, IL 61036
815-777-0557

Owners/Operators:
Country Inns, Inc.
(Pam and Bill Lozeau)

This 16-room mansion on Highway 20 is known locally for lunches and dinners in the parlor dining rooms and for dancing at the "Back in Tyme" lounge next door (open Friday and Saturday nights only). Upstairs are five guest rooms.

Nelson Stillman, owner of Stillman's Dry Goods Store, built the house in 1858. It was home to four family members and five servants. Ulysses S. Grant and his wife dined here. At one time, Stillman owned the entire hillside.

Stillman also is remembered for starting one of the first public schools in Galena by renting a home and hiring a teacher on his own. He believed education should not be a privilege just for the rich.

In 1900, the mansion was sold for back taxes of $500. From the '30s to '60s, it was Sunny Hill Nursing Home, and a first-floor kitchen (now the bar) was added.

After serving as an Italian restaurant at one point, new owners purchased the mansion in the mid-'70s, converting the building to a restaurant and inn, and adding parking lots and the adjacent bar. In November 1985 it was bought by Pam and Bill Lozeau, who had been in Galena for a decade and owned an antique shop downtown, and Bill had started a '50s club in Dubuque. They now live on the third floor.

This is one of three properties owned by Pam and Bill under the name Country Inns, Inc. (The Cloran Mansion is described in the Galena Area section.)

Rooms and Rates: Five - All upstairs with queen beds, antiques or reproductions, private baths, color cable TVs, and radios. Examples include: #5 is former servant's quarters, has canopy bed, sofa bed, gas fireplace, small refrigerator, done in peach, blue and green, bath with tub/shower - $95. #4 has blue bedspread, wing chairs, gas fireplace, marble-topped furniture, large Victorian print wallpaper, sink in room, bath with shower only - $80. #2 has peach, gold and green floral wallpaper, oriental rug, antique chairs, bath with shower only - $65. Rates are single or double. Add tax.

Meals: Continental breakfast is placed in the entry way for guests to eat in their rooms or outside on the patio 8-11. It includes sweet rolls and muffins.

Dates Open: Year 'round

Smoking: Yes (owners do)

Children: Over 12

Pets: No

Handicapped Access: No

A/C: Central

Other/Group Uses: Bus tours for lunches and dinner, small weddings and receptions.

Location: Located in East Galena, with parking off Highway 20, across the street from Grant's House Historic Site.

Deposit: $40 per room per night or confirmation by credit card

Payment: Cash, personal or traveler's checks, VISA, MasterCard or AMEX

Belle Aire Mansion Guest House

11410 Route 20 West   Owners/Operators:
Galena, IL 61036   Lorraine and Jan Svec
815-777-0893

The Scadden brothers built this Federal-style home, starting it in a small log cabin on their farm. Over the years, the house was expanded, the last addition being built in 1879. One of the brothers later built the house next door.

The mansion stayed in the Scadden family until the mid-1960s, then was sold to a couple with 10 children who needed the large home. They did much of the renovation, then sold it in 1981 to a couple who opened a B&B. Lorraine and Jan Svec and Lorraine's sister and brother-in-law, Lyn and Mike Cook, bought the operating business in August 1987, after Lorraine had been bitten by the B&B bug.

Lorraine worked in the post office for 17 years "before retiring to start a family." She looked into starting a B&B before their second child was born. They looked for property in Fox Lake, Ill., where they were living, "but nothing pleased us. Then we came to Galena for a weekend." They came with the Cooks, found the B&B, talked Cooks into the venture, went back and sold their homes. It turned out so well that Lyn and Mike have their own B&B in town, Brierwreath Manor.

Svecs have remodeled bathrooms and added a new one, but otherwise found the large house in good condition. Jan, who works in the Galena Post Office, counts Belle Aire as his second job and is the resident handyman.

Daughter Bryony and son Josh will share their toys, games and baby supplies with visiting children. The living room is also a family game room, with some modern furniture, a piano, TV, VCR and tapes. There are two verandas, and the one off the top floor has a porch swing. Tea, coffee and hot chocolate are available anytime in the dining room. Coffee is available upstairs at 6 a.m.

Rooms and Rates: Four - All upstairs with some antiques and some modern furniture. The Blue Room has king brass bed, antique sofa, done in blue and white, bath with tub/shower - $70. Canopy Suite has a sitting room with country sofa bed, bedroom with double white-eyelet canopy bed, done in pink and white, bath with tub/shower - $80. Victorian Room has double antique carved walnut bed, marble-top furniture, shares bath with Ruthie's Room - $60. Ruthie's Room has rose wallpaper, double brass bed, ice cream table, shared bath has wainscoting, clawfoot tub/shower - $60. Rates are double; single, $5 less. Weekdays, $5 less. Seniors, $5 less. Each additional adult, $10. Two-night minimum stay required holiday weekends. Add tax.

Meals: Breakfast is served in the dining room 8-10. It may include fresh fruit, homemade date-nut or banana breads, a breakfast meat, and scrambled eggs, pancakes, waffles, French toast or a souffle.

Dates Open: Year 'round

Smoking: On verandas only

Children: Welcome (cribs and cots available)

Pets: No

Handicapped Access: No

A/C: Window units

Other/Group Uses: Weddings up to 60, meetings up to 10.

Location: Main Street, 3 miles via Franklin Street. Located on Highway 20 west of town.

Deposit: First night's lodging or confirmation by credit card

Payment: Cash, personal or traveler's checks, VISA or MasterCard

The Cloran Mansion

1237 Franklin St.
Galena, IL 61036
815-777-0583

Owners/Operators:
   Country Inns, Inc.
   (Pam and Bill Lozeau)
Innkeepers: JoEllen and Bob Lozeau

Located off Highway 20 across from the middle school, this brick mansion served as the centerpiece of a 250-acre farm. It was built in 1880 by John Cloran, a farmer and grocer whose store operated at 115 N. Main from 1900-17.

The building was the American Legion Post in the '50s and '60s, then was a private residence, and then was turned into apartments.

In December 1988, Lozeaus bought the building and brothers Bob and Bill started work to convert it to a guest house. "We're both sort of jacks of all trades, so we did as much as we could ourselves," Bob said.

Barnwood paneling in the double entry way was removed and the entryway rebuilt. The house was replumbed, rewired and installed with a new furnace and central air conditioning. Rooms were left in their original spaces, but bricked up windows were replaced, new closets and bathrooms were created, and salvaged mantels were refinished and installed. The house was completely carpeted.

JoEllen and Bob, who both work at Stillman's Country Inn, live on the first floor, and guests may knock on their door if assistance is needed.

This is one of three properties owned by Pam and Bill Lozeau under the name Country Inns, Inc. (Stillman's Country Inn is described in the Galena section.)

Rooms and Rates: Five - All upstairs with antiques or reproductions, private baths, color cable TVs and radios. #5 has a king brass bed, Eastlake chairs, mirror-manteled gas fireplace; guests climb the stairs to the top of the turret, which is the double whirlpool room with large mirrors - $110. #1 has a queen bed, fireplace, is done in beige and peach, has double whirlpool/shower - $95. #2 is small room with double brass bed, done in beige and blue, bath with tub/shower - $55. #3 is former kitchen, has knotty pine cathedral ceiling with fan, fireplace, done in mint green and beige; bath is bright, brick-walled sun porch, double whirlpool/shower - $95. #4 has wicker furniture, queen bed, ceiling fan, done in rose and green floral, bath with tub/shower - $65. Two-night minimum stay required weekends except for rooms #2 and #4. Add tax.

Meals: Continental breakfast is placed in the entry way for guests to eat in their rooms or outside on patio 8-11. It includes sweet rolls and muffins.

Dates Open: Year 'round

Smoking: Yes (innkeepers do)

Children: Over 12

Pets: No

Handicapped Access: No

A/C: Central

Other/Group Uses: No

Nearby: Main Street, 1.1 miles via Franklin Street. Dairy Dreem cafe on corner.

Location: From Highway 20, turn south at the corner by the Dairy Dreem and school. Mansion is across the street from the middle school.

Deposit: $40 per room per night or confirmation by credit card

Payment: Cash, personal or traveler's checks, VISA, MasterCard or AMEX

The Cunningham House

110 Market St.

Platteville, WI 53818

608-348-5532

Owners/Operators:

Arletta and Jud Giese

The name of Dr. Wilson Cunningham might not mean much to most people, but if you ever have bone grafts, or know someone who has, you may owe him a debt of gratitude. Cunningham was a pioneer surgeon, one of the first to use animal bones in transplants to humans. He also waged his own type of germ warfare, installing sinks in every bedroom of the house for increased cleanliness. And he's remembered locally for running his own car as an ambulance, "and he never stopped for a stoplight," said Jud Giese.

Cunningham had this house on the downtown "square" built in 1907. He and his wife raised three children here. He lived here until 1962 when he died at the age of 90. The Grant County Historical Society then used the home for more than two decades as its museum.

The Cunningham Museum moved to Lancaster, 15 miles away, some 10 years after the furnace quit working. When Gieses bought the home in 1987, they had broken radiators, inadequate plumbing, an attic full of bats and a basement with coal dust with which to contend. Woodwork was painted and leaded glass covered.

But they saw the home as "well worth rescuing," said Arletta, who sits on the Downtown Revitalization Committee and plunged into much of the work herself before Jud moved to Platteville full-time. "Jud wanted to retire and we started looking at the housing market here. We had one daughter here and we'd come out to see her, and we loved the area." A realtor suggested opening a B&B.

With new utilities, mostly-stripped woodwork and new wallpaper, and no bats, the B&B opened in May 1988. The first prominent guest was former U.S. Senator Shirley Chisholm, who spoke at the University of Wisconsin - Platteville, and ended up staying an extra day to relax.

Homemade gingersnaps are placed in rooms before bed, and guests are free to use the large living room downstairs.

Rooms and Rates: Three - All on second floor with sinks. All share two baths with tubs/showers. Sylvia Room has two twin beds, done in country blue and white with matching linens and wallpaper, skirted sink. Debbie Room has twin brass beds, mint green and rose decor, down comforters and electric blankets. Cindy Room has double bed, peach down comforter and floral wallpaper. $40 single, $45 double. Each additional person on rollaway cot, $10. Add tax.

Meals: Breakfast is served in the dining room at a time arranged the night before. It may include baked French toast, cheese strata or omelettes, breakfast meat, homemade banana muffins and fresh-squeezed juice.

Dates Open: Year 'round

Smoking: In parlor only

Children: "You bet"

Pets: No (deaf cat in residence)

Handicapped Access: No

A/C: Central

Other/Group Uses: Catered luncheons, parties and receptions, meetings.

Nearby: Galena, 25 miles. Dubuque, 22 miles. Park, across the street. University of Wisconsin - Platteville (Shakespeare festival), 6 blocks. Rollo Jamison Museum and Mining Museum, Stone Cottage historic home, 7 blocks. Chicago Bears summer training camp (free scrimmage games), 8 blocks.

Location: Located on north side of city square. Detailed map sent.

Deposit: Full amount in advance

Payment: Cash, personal or traveler's checks only

Log Cabin Guest House

1161 W. Chetlain Lane
Galena, IL 61036
815-777-2845

Owners/Operators:
Linda and Scott Ettleman

Three original log cabins — the kind that were built of planed logs and chinking, not from pre-cut kits — have been moved to this site, and a servants' quarters above a garage renovated to serve as private guest houses at this three-acre country home.

General Augustus Chetlain, one of Galena's Civil War generals, grew into adulthood here. His father, Louis Chetlain, built the house in 1832 to move his family here from Wisconsin, where he was the liaison between Indian and white leaders for the Wisconsin Territory. Louis Chetlain feared attack by Black Hawk, and Galena had built a stockade, to which many white settlers from the surrounding area flocked. Black Hawk did not attack Galena, but the Chetlain family stayed.

When the Civil War was declared and Lincoln called for troops to fight for the Union, Augustus Chetlain emerged as a spokesman for a Galena group when they went to Springfield to enlist. He was commissioned a captain right away, on May 2, to lead the first Volunteer Company of Galena.

After the war, Grant appointed him as ambassador to Belgium. A book Chetlain wrote, "Recollection of 70 Years," suggested they had a falling out which never was completely patched up. Chetlain lived out his life in Chicago.

The main cabin on this site was moved from a farm between here and East Dubuque, then reassembled. Scott Ettleman moved and reassembled the two smaller cabins, which were two buildings covered with barnwood from Potosi, Wis.

Rooms and Rates: Four private cottages - Each with private bath with shower only. Servants' House has sitting room with color TV and couch, done in blue and cream striped country wallpaper; in bedroom, one queen brass bed, antique white iron crib. Window air conditioner, refrigerator, small microwave, children welcome - $50. Main Cabin has double bed, limestone fireplace, color TV downstairs, two rope beds for children upstairs, window air conditioner, children welcome - $65. Rates are single or double. $5 extra for families. Each additional adult, $10. Cabins 2 and 3 for adults only, each have queen beds, huge limestone fireplace, couch downstairs, central air, bath with shower only and double whirlpool built in loft-like upstairs - $75 weekdays, $85 weekends. Two-night minimum stay required weekends. Add tax.

Meals: Not served. A coffee maker is provided in each guest house. Small refrigerators and microwaves in some cabins (see above).

Dates Open: Year 'round

Smoking: "Not encouraged"

Children: In two cabins (see above)

Pets: No

Handicapped Access: No

A/C: Yes (see above)

Other/Group Uses: No

Location: Main Street, 1.8 miles via Franklin Street. Located off of Highway 20 west of town (watch for signs on highway).

Deposit: First night's lodging or confirmation by credit card

Payment: Cash, personal or traveler's checks, VISA or MasterCard

Maple Lane Country Inn

3114 Rush Creek Road
Stockton, IL 61085
815-947-3773

Owners/Operators:
Elizabeth and Carson Herring

It's easy to see why Swiss Colony in Monroe, Wis., hires Elizabeth Herring to deal with Christmas customers who have had their cheese gift boxes lost in the mail or their Dobosh Tortes smashed in. "They get me on the phone and they are *mad,*" said Elizabeth with a giggle. Chances are, they're not mad for long.

Elizabeth and Carson bought this dairy farm in 1954. Started in the late 1890s by the Hogan family, the house, first built with eight rooms, now has 17.

Elizabeth opened the guest house back in 1957, about two years after seeing an ad in the Chicago Tribune for a booklet on New York state farm vacations. "I wondered why there were not farm vacations here for people who wanted to take their children to a farm." She advertised her place, offering a room, three meals a day, entertainment, and pick up from train or bus. "The first year we had seven families here for one week each. The next year we had 14 families. The next year we had 21 families who wanted to come and we were sleeping in the cellar!"

Until 1977, the business grew so that they had 20 riding horses, a commercial kitchen and an in-ground, 20 x 50-foot outdoor swimming pool. They added housing units in back. "Then we just flatfooted stopped for about eight years." The units were converted to apartments, but eventually Stockton provided all the necessary rental units in the area. The farm land is rented to other farmers, one of whom has cattle, but the farm animals are gone, too.

"I wanted to do a B&B for a long time. It was in the back of my mind all the time," Elizabeth said. In 1985, Herrings opened four guest rooms in their large home, which was redecorated in the '50s. Guests may still use the swimming pool, the bikes, or the sauna and four-person whirlpool in a separate building. Herrings have been trained in the art of Swedish massage, and massages also are available for an additional cost in the separate building. For guests' use, the family room has a fireplace and living room has a piano and drum set, which Herrings might be talked into playing.

Rooms and Rates: Four - All upstairs with color TV, all with some modern furniture, sculptured carpet and '50s decor. Garden Suite and Rose Suite each have double bed, sitting room, bath with shower only - $55. Flower and Corner Rooms each have double beds, share a bath with tub/shower - $45. Rates are double; single, $5 less. Each additional person, $10. Add tax.

Meals: Breakfast is served in the dining rooms at a time arranged the night before. Guests have a choice of fruits, homemade coffeecake, bread or muffins, and eggs any style, pancakes or French toast and a breakfast meat.

Dates open: Year 'round

Smoking: Not encouraged

Children: Yes (BYO cribs)

Pets: No

Handicapped Access: No

A/C: Window units

Other/Group Uses: Sauna/fitness center building seats up to 30 for meetings; dining room seats up to 60.

Nearby: Galena, 22 miles. Fishing for small-mouth bass in Rush Creek, 2 blocks. Restaurants, antique shops in Stockton, 5 miles.

Location: From Highway 20, turn south at sign at Hatton Road. At intersection with Rush Creek Road, turn left and follow signs. Map sent (and needed).

Deposit: $15 per room

Payment: Cash, personal or traveler's checks only

Noni's Bed & Breakfast

516 W. Main St.
Warren, IL 61087
815-745-2045 (home)
815-745-2000 (work)

Owner/Operator:
    Naomi "Noni" McCool

This Main Street home is believed to have been built in 1857, but little is known about it in town. When owner Noni McCool worked at the local historical society (now defunct), "someone brought us some postcards that showed the house. It was really Victorian, with gingerbread and a porch and a bay window off the side."

The home changed hands several times over the years, with a man named Burrows owning it the longest, from 1915-1945. Burrows was in the lumber business.

At some time before she and her late husband, a dentist, bought it in 1950, the exterior had been "remuddled" and those pretty details removed. Noni also knows that the Queen Anne home next door was a funeral home, and at one time the back lots were jointly planted with a large potato crop by the two neighbors.

Noni opened the B&B in 1987 after sitting on the country tourism board and learning about B&Bs. "In the fall of the year there wasn't room for everybody (coming to Galena). I thought that I've got a big house and there isn't any reason I couldn't do something like this."

If there would be a reason, she said, it would be that she works full-time as a bookkeeper, so the B&B is mostly a weekend hobby. "I'm thinking that if I retire in a couple years, maybe I'll concentrate on it." Now, she redecorates one room a year to return the historic feel.

Guests have the use of the living room, with modern furniture, green carpet and gold walls, plus the library, dining room and sun porch. "I don't care if they want to put some pop in the fridge — it's OK with me," she said.

Rooms and Rates: Three - All upstairs sharing a bath with tub/shower. There is a half-bath downstairs that Noni also uses. Front room has a double four-poster bed, navy "country" wallpaper, white woodwork, lace curtains. Second room has a double bed, done in mauve, beige and grey. Third room is for "overflow" and rented mostly to children, has a twin bed and a crib, modern furniture, done in gold. $30 single, $40 double. No charge for young children. Multiple-night discount. Add tax.

Meals: Breakfast is served in the dining room or on the sun porch at a time arranged the night before. It may include fresh fruit compote, muffins, rolls or breads, and eggs benedict, omelettes or strata.

Dates Open: Year 'round

Smoking: Not in guest rooms

Children: "Well behaved"

Pets: No

Handicapped Access: No

A/C: No

Other/Group Uses: No

Nearby: Meridian Park (located on the 90th principal meridian) with swimming pool, tennis, 2 blocks. Antique shops and restaurant, Warren Cheese Company retail store and window for viewing cheese-making until 10:30 a.m., 4 blocks. Apple River Canyon State Park, hiking, trout fishing and picnicking, 6 miles.

Location: Galena, 35 miles. Take Highway 20 to State Highway 78, north on 78 to Warren. Or take Stagecoach Trail between Warren and Galena.

Deposit: $20 per room

Payment: Cash, personal or traveler's checks only

Pat's Country Guest Home

5148 Highway 20 West   Owners/Operators:
Galena, IL 61036   Pat and John Tyson
815-777-1030

What the Hansen family built as a modest, three-bedroom farmhouse at the turn of the century, the Tyson family has turned into a expansive B&B, office and home, all spread out a comfortable distance from each other.

John Tyson guesses that Hansens were herdsmen because the soil on the 46 acres at the entrance to the Galena Territory resort is rocky and unsuitable for farming. The original farmhouse consisted of what is now the kitchen and dining room downstairs and two B&B bedrooms and a bath upstairs.

The living room originally was a cabin from somewhere else on the property that was moved up and added on, though uninsulated. Side rooms were added on to that. The sun porch and a separate wing, where Pat and John sleep and which houses John's office for his woodworking business, were added last.

Tysons are the third owners, with the J. Walter Schmidd family coming in between. Pat and John bought the home in 1967 as a weekend place. It wasn't long before Pat and the kids would stay all week and John would come out from Chicago on the weekends. In the mid-1980s, John sold his interest in a bowling alley and construction business and moved to Galena permanently. In his shop next door he makes custom furniture.

Pat opened the B&B in 1987. "I had a son in real estate who suggested it," she said, and she was egged on by friends who enjoyed her cooking and knew she had the extra bedrooms. John prefers to leave the B&B business to Pat.

The home was restored and improved over the years, including replacing two floor furnaces with new heating and plumbing and rewiring. The home is decorated in antiques, John's handmade furniture and country pieces.

Guests are welcome to use the living room with color TV and the sun porch, populated with plants and a woodstove. There are also benches, a yard swing and a patio, plus guests are free to hike, x-c ski, bird watch or picnic on the 46 acres.

Rooms and Rates: Two - Both upstairs with double antique beds, shared bath with clawfoot tub only (shower available in downstairs bathroom). One room has white iron bed, wicker rocker, done in yellow and blue - $45. Other room has Jenny Lind spool bed, family heirloom furniture, done in pink and cream - $50. Rates are double; single, $5 less. Two-night minimum stay required peak-season weekends. Add tax.

Meals: Continental breakfast is served in the dining room at 8:30. It may include fresh fruit, a cheese plate, homemade muffins, scones and fruit bread.

Dates Open: Year 'round

Smoking: No

Children: No

Pets: No (lap dogs on premises)

Handicapped Access: No

A/C: Window units

Other/Group Uses: No

Nearby: X-c skiing on grounds. Adjacent to Galena Territory resort, which has golf, riding, x-c skiing and restaurants open to the public.

Location: Main Street, 7 miles. Located east of Galena on Highway 20; 100 feet east of Galena Territory entrance.

Deposit: Confirmation by credit card

Payment: Cash, personal or traveler's checks, VISA, MasterCard or AMEX

Pine Hollow Inn*

4700 N. Council Hill Rd.
Galena, IL 61036
815-777-1071

Owners/Operators:
Sally and Larry Priske

Samuel Hughlett once owned this valley, having two smelting furnaces serving the lead mines up the hills. Hughlett also had a huge clapboard home built just across the trail from where this inn stands today. Foundations from the smelting buildings dot the valley, and an archeological dig a few years back turned up artifacts.

"There are all kinds of holes all over the place. In fact, a coyote den used to be a mining hole," said Sally Priske.

Priskes bought 110 acres of Hughlett's valley and hills in 1984. They started a Christmas tree farm; you can cut your own in 1993 or so. They also decided to build a B&B. Larry, who teaches technical courses for John Deere in Dubuque, brainstormed it as another way to diversify and be able to stay in Galena.

One of the reasons a B&B was appealing was to be able to have others enjoy the property, they said. Andy, the golden retriever, assists by taking willing guests over hill and dale, often ignoring his owners for the repeated opportunity of being engaged as tour guide. Wildflower, morel and wildlife-tracking weekends are planned by Priskes.

Priskes constructed the country house and opened in February 1989. They live in another house on the property and come over to serve breakfast and assist guests. A stream flows nearby and benches dot the substantial porch.

Guests can use the refrigerator, stocked with a complimentary beverage, and microwave. Wood is stacked by each brick fireplace.

Rooms and Rates: Five - All with country decor, fireplaces, ceiling fans, queen four-poster beds, private baths. #1, 2 and 5 are downstairs with small side porches. #1 is done in blue and yellow, has sofa bed, double whirlpool and separate shower. #2 is in purple, has duck motif wallpaper, double whirlpool with separate shower. #5 is in dark green and blue, has ceiling beams with hanging baskets, stained glass window, wing chairs, bath with clawfoot tub/shower. #3 and #4 are upstairs with vaulted, beamed ceilings and skylights, and baths with tub/shower. #3 is in cream and light blue. #4 is in rose and cream, has view of hillside. $85 weekends, $75 weekdays. Rates are single or double. Midweek, multiple-night discounts. Two-night minimum stay required weekends. Add tax.

Meals: Continental breakfast is served in the kitchen 8:30-9. It may include homemade cinnamon rolls, coffeecake and/or muffins, and fresh fruit.

Dates Open: Year 'round   **Smoking:** No

Children: Over 12   **Pets:** No

Handicapped Access: No   **A/C:** Central

Other/Group Uses: Bike tours, wildflower weekends, guided nature hikes.

Nearby: Less than two miles from downtown Galena.

Location: Go north on Main Street (it turns into Dewey). Cross river and turn left on Council Hill road; turn left again at sign to driveway. Detailed map sent.

Deposit: First night's lodging or confirmation by credit card

Payment: Cash, personal or traveler's checks, VISA or MasterCard

Wisconsin House Stagecoach Inn

2105 E. Main St.   Owners/Operators:
Hazel Green, WI 53811   Betha and John Mueller
608-854-2233

Betha and John Mueller opened their inn in 1985 after owning a B&B for three years in Galena. Not that they weren't having a good time in Galena, nine miles away. "We always wanted an original old inn and this was for sale," said Betha. The inn was built in 1846 as one of many stagecoach stops along the route to Galena, then a booming lead mining and transportation hub.

Hazel Green had mines of its own. In 1853, Jefferson Crawford, who owned several area mines, bought the inn as a private home. The millionaire often hosted his friend, young Ulysses S. Grant, who stayed when selling leather goods for his father's store in Galena. Grant was so close to the family that he helped with funeral arrangements for Crawford. The inn stayed in the family until 1958, when "Miss Helen," Jefferson's granddaughter, died. It even withstood an 1876 tornado.

After a few more owners and a stint as an apartment house, the inn was restored by Muellers, who added bathrooms and decorated it in country decor worthy of features in Country Living and Midwest Living Magazines.

Betha and John grew up on neighboring farms in the next county, childhood sweethearts who played in a band together and raised eight children, four of them foster children. They have farmed, run a supper club and operated a state park concession, all close to home. Now they have an antique and gift shop at the inn.

Though the decor is flawless, this place is as comfortable as an old shoe. John, who's quick with a joke, says nothing is off-limits in the house, including the kitchen. But their meals, served at the 16-foot dining room table, easily fill up travelers. Local red and white wine produced for their label is served at dinners.

Rooms and Rates: Nine - All beds have antique quilts and rooms are done in picture-perfect country decor. Jefferson Crawford Room has double ruffled-canopy bed, private bath with tub/shower - $65. Dr. Percival Room is done in blues, double antique bed, private bath with shower only - $55. Miss Helen's Room ($45) has two twin beds and antique toys, shares bath with clawfoot tub and shower with Grant Room ($50) and Indian ($40) Room. Norwegian and Swiss rooms in new addition each have private bath with tub/shower - $65 each. Mississippi Room has dormers, half-bath only - $65. Handyman's Room has shared bath downstairs - $40. Rates are double; single, $5 less. Second night, $5 less. Off-season discounts. Add tax.

Meals: Breakfast is served in the kitchen or dining room at a time arranged the night before, for guests or by reservation, including bacon, sausage or ham, eggs or pancakes, potatoes and fruit. Family-style supper served Friday and Saturday by reservation and other times for groups; price fixed at $15.95 and one entree item, plus house wine, recipes from country inns. Betha and John provide entertainment.

Dates Open: Year 'round   **Smoking:** Not in bedrooms   **Pets:** No

Children: "Well-behaved"   **Handicapped Access:** No   **A/C:** Window

Other/Group Uses: Bike tours, small meetings, lunches or dinners up to 22.

Nearby: Main Street, 9 miles. Dubuque, 13 miles. X-c ski trail and Hazel Green walking tour. Platteville (Mining Museum, Rollo Jameson Museum and lead mine tour), 14 miles. Two lead mine tours, 5 miles and 15 miles.

Location: From Highway 20, take Highway 84 at Fran's Cafe up to Hazel Green; inn is at the corner of County Road W and Main Street.

Deposit: First night's lodging or confirmation by credit card

Payment: Cash, personal or traveler's checks, VISA or MasterCard

Welcome to Dubuque

Dubuque, Iowa, used to be thought of as a blue-collar town where meat packing was the only thing happening.

Today, Dubuque has become a tourist destination. Finally appreciated for its grand architecture and high limestone bluffs overlooking the Mississippi River, and with attractions of its own, more and more visitors are finding out about what Dubuque has to offer. In addition, it's only about a 20-minute drive to Galena.

To B&B travelers, Dubuque does itself proud. The B&Bs in downtown Dubuque are the grandest of the grand homes. That's partly because to open a B&B in Dubuque, it has to be located in one of the town's five historic districts.

So far, innkeepers have chosen to find diamond-in-the-rough mansions that ranged from needing lots of work to nearly falling apart and needing super-major work. When they are restored to their original luster, they truly sparkle like the treasures that they once again are. One mansion has an entry hall paneled in rosewood. Another has mosaic tile that stretches all around a wrap-around porch. A third has curved leaded glass inlaid into the buffet to reflect the light of gas chandeliers. Another has a three-sided fireplace, one side of which has enough cherry fretwork to satisfy any homeowner.

The attitude that these pioneering innkeepers have about sharing their renewed jewels with their communities and with travelers is remarkable as well. It was best summed up by Madi Schlarman, who, with her family, bought and restored the massive Captain Merry House in East Dubuque, Illinois, putting in years of exhausting labor. Madi said, "This is our home, but it is East Dubuque's heritage."

And what a heritage it is. The men who built these houses were the movers and shakers of the Dubuque area: a wagon works owner, the founder of five banks, a granary owner, the largest wholesale grocery distributor in the Midwest, the owner of a department store known as "the Macy's of Dubuque," and three owners or partners in lumber companies.

While the two lodgings outside of town, Juniper Hill Farm and Oak Crest Cottage, are not mansions, they are highly recommended and would be an asset to any community. Both are charming and the hosts spent lots of time and TLC on decorating and renovating run-down buildings.

Extraordinary mansions-turned-inns are not the only architectural discoveries here. St. Luke's United Methodist Church, built in 1896, has Tiffany glass windows. The Mathias Ham House, an 1857 Italianate Villa-style mansion, is open as an historic site. The Grand Opera House, built in 1889-90, has a summer repertory theater and a resident ghost. The ornate Ryan House, built in 1873, is now open to the public as a fine restaurant.

The courthouse and jail, City Hall, public library, the German Bank and Five Flags Theater all are on the National Register of Historic Places. The Five Flags Theater was modeled after Parisian theaters when it was built in 1910, and is today restored and part of the Five Flags Civic Center.

Like Galena, Dubuque was founded as a lead mining town. At various times, Dubuque has flown five different flags over the city, those of England, Spain, the U.S. and two of France. The boom that resulted from the lead, lumber and location on the Mississippi River led to prosperity and construction of magnificent buildings.

Today, Dubuque has 65,000 people, three colleges, two seminaries, and one great candy shop, Betty Jane's (on Main Street near Town Clock Plaza; try the Gremlins, "turtles" by any other name).

Dubuque also has:

Sidewheeler William M. Black - If you can't take a cruise, you can tour the pilothouse, staterooms, crews quarters, galley and engine room of a 277-foot paddelwheeler at the Ice Harbor. Open summers only; $4.

Woodward Riverboat Museum - is also at Second Street and the Ice Harbor. It is open daily 10 a.m. - 6:30 p.m. May through October and 10 a.m. - 4 p.m. Tuesday through Sunday the rest of the year. The museum explains not only riverboats, but lead mining, fresh-water clamming, native fish species and other Mississippi facts; $4.

Riverboat Rides - At Ice Harbor near the Highway 20 bridge, you can catch narrated sightseeing cruises, dinner and dance cruises, brunch cruises and lock cruises May through October.

Dubuque Greyhound Park - has been getting lots of attention since it opened in 1985 right near downtown. Races start at 1 p.m. for matinees, 7:30 p.m. for evening racing. The season runs April-November, but check dates for exact racing times.

Riverboat Gambling - If a day at the track is not enough for you, you'll get a chance to gamble on riverboats starting in April 1991. The Iowa legislature passed Mississippi Riverboat gambling in 1989, then the Illinois legislature OK'd it to begin in January 1991. That may mean East Dubuque, Ill., will get a four-month jump on the Dubuque folks. At this writing, questions on where to catch the boat, when and for how much were premature. Call the Dubuque Visitors Bureau.

Fenelon Place Elevator - Also known as the Fourth Street Elevator, located at 512 Fenelon Place on top of the bluff, Fourth Street below it. Billed as "the world's shortest, steepest scenic railway," the cable car lifts passengers 296 feet up the bluff between Fenelon Place and Fourth Street, at an elevation of 189 feet. There's a view of the Tri-State Area. Open April through November only.

Antiquing/Shopping - Near the Elevator is Cable Car Square, running along Fourth and Bluff streets. Antiques, gifts, quilts and other specialties are sold in about 25 shops in historic buildings, and restaurants are included, as well. There is good antiquing (generally less expensive than downtown Galena) in other areas of town, too.

Farmer's Market - Not to be missed at 13th Street and Iowa Streets every Saturday morning May through November.

Eagle Point Park and Zebulon Pike Lock and Dam (#11) - The park overlooks Lock and Dam #11, with good views of the Tri-State Area, as well. Free tours of the 4,818-foot dam are available Sundays at 2 p.m. Memorial Day through Labor Day.

Heritage Nature Trail - This is a 26-mile biking, hiking, x-c skiing and snowmobiling trail between Sageville and Dyersville (location of the "Field of Dreams" movie farm). It is on an old railroad track, so the grade is gentle.

Victorian Progressive Dinner and House Tour - Mansion-lovers will want to take in this unique event every Friday at 6:15 p.m. June through October (other times by arrangement). You travel by motorcoach to the Ham House, Redstone Inn, Ryan House and Stout House, where you tour the mansions and consume a portion of a five-course meal, about a five-hour event. This is operated through the Dubuque County Historical Society (1-319-557-9545), and reservations are required, of course. Cost is about $30 per person.

Walking/Driving Tours - The Historical Society also has three 30-minute walking tours and a driving tour of historic churches in the Tri-State Area.

Downhill Skiing - Sundown Ski Area is located about eight miles west of Dubuque. It has 17 runs with a 475 foot vertical drop and it makes snow.

Mines of Spain - This 1,380-acre area includes the E.B. Lyons Prairie Woodland Preserve (37 acres with an interpretive center and hiking trails) and the Julien Dubuque Monument (on the National Historic Register). It includes the old lead mining area to which Dubuque had exclusive operating rights under the Spanish government. It's about five miles from downtown Dubuque.

There also are numerous special art shows, home tours, music and food festivals and other special events throughout the year. Contact the **Dubuque Convention and Visitors Bureau, 1-800-79-VISIT** (1-800-798-4748).

Driving times, depending on destination, speed and road conditions to Dubuque from:

> Chicago - 3 to 4 hours
> Minneapolis-St. Paul - 5 to 6 hours
> St. Louis - 6 to 7 hours
> Madison - less than 90 minutes
> Milwaukee - about 3 hours
> Galena - 20 minutes

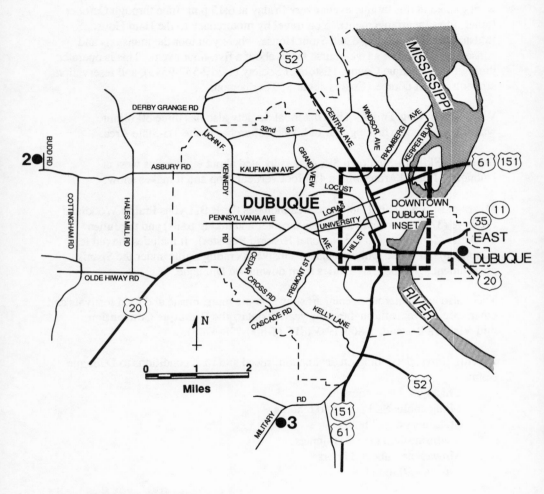

❖ Nearby Dubuque

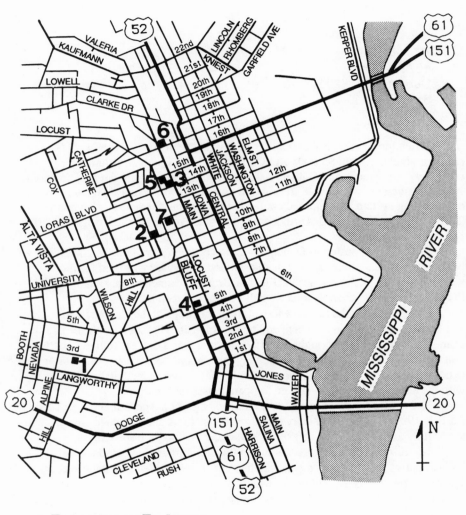

❖ Downtown Dubuque

Collier Mansion

1072 W. Third
Dubuque, IA 52001
319-588-2130

Owners/Operators:
Mary and Paul Fitzgerald

When lumberman Robert Collier built this Queen Anne home in 1897, the cost was an exhorbitant $5,000. But Collier, a partner in the huge lumber company Carr, Adams and Collier, was able to afford and obtain the best, including African mahogany woodwork. It originally was built with a new-fangled air conditioning system that pumped cool water throughout the house. The house has 21 rooms, some with rounded windows and rounded rooms, and the original marble bathrooms are still intact.

The home is located in Dubuque's Langworthy Preservation District, amid other grand homes. It has a large, lush backyard. The yard was used for the wedding and graduation scenes in "Field of Dreams," filmed in the area in 1988. (The star, Kevin Costner, shot basketball here in between takes.)

Fitzgeralds are the third owners of the home outside the Collier family. A local jeweler owned it in between, and he is responsible for some of the ornate chandeliers. Fitzgeralds bought it in 1976 when it was a duplex, to live in half and rent the other. "We just came on a Sunday open house because we had nothing else to do and wanted to look at old houses," said Mary, who immediately fell in love with the house. (They no longer go to open houses on Sundays.)

Mary, who teaches nursing, and Paul, an educational consultant, opened the B&B in 1987. "We've been on two or three house tours and people always wanted to see it," she explained. "The people who come (to stay) are special."

The original stained-glass pattern in the dining room bay window, the built-in buffet and the stairway all match; some of it is leaded and some is copper. The music parlor has a grand piano, which guests may use, and Wedgewood candelabras. A large, screened side porch also is for guests' use.

Rooms and Rates: Four - Only three of which usually are rented on one night, all upstairs on second floor. Queen Anne Room has double lace canopy bed, bay window, done in beige and blue, bath with tub/hand-held shower - $70. Balcony Room has double bed, French doors, done in burgundy and beige, shares large bath with tub/shower - $60. Wedgewood Room has sleigh bed, carved wood wainscoting, shares bath - $65. Sometimes fourth room is rented, has a double four-poster, half-canopy bed, done in rust and tan, shares bath - $50. Rates are double; single, $5 less. Each additional adult, $5. Midweek discounts. Add tax.

Meals: Breakfast is served in the dining room at a time arranged the night before. It may include sweet rolls, Iowa ham or sausage, and fresh fruit crepes, pancakes, a breakfast casserole or puff pancake.

Dates Open: Year 'round

Smoking: On porch only

Children: Yes

Pets: No

Handicapped Access: No

A/C: Window units

Other/Group Uses: Meetings, weddings, parties, catered events up to 60.

Nearby: Fenelon Place Elevator, 4 blocks. Riverboat rides, 10 blocks. Greyhound track, 1.5 miles. Woodward Riverboat Museum, 10 blocks. Sundown Ski Area, 7 miles. Heritage Nature Trail, 4 miles. Downtown Galena, 14 miles.

Location: Go up the bluff on Highway 20 (Dodge Street) to corner of Alpine. Turn right to the corner of West Third. Turn right on Third. Map sent.

Deposit: $25 per room or confirmation by credit card

Payment: Cash, personal or traveler's checks, VISA or MasterCard

The Hancock House

1105 Grove Terrace
Dubuque, IA 52001
319-557-8989

Owners/Operators:
Julie and Jim Gross
Innkeeper: Terri Westmark

From the front of this blufftop mansion, every window has a view that looks like a scenic photograph of downtown Dubuque. The 1891 Queen Anne, listed on the National Register of Historic Places, was built by Charles T. Hancock, once the largest wholesale grocery distributor in the Midwest. Hancock also was listed as president of the Iowa Gold Mining Company, had an insurance company, participated in horse racing and was on the Methodist church board.

The 7,200-square-foot house is perhaps most remarkable for its three-sided fireplace, which has won design awards. The parlor face has intricate cherry fretwork, and it won a blue ribbon in the 1893 World's Fair in Chicago. Also, an original mural on oatmeal paper lines the dining room walls.

Julie, formerly an executive secretary, and Jim, a realtor who manages commerical real estate, have three young children, love old homes, and "we weren't content in our little ranch house," Julie said. They bought the nine-unit apartment building in March 1985 and began to undo 25 years of its life as rental units. "We did 60 to 70 percent of the work ourselves," Julie said, and it took them until August 1987 to open the B&B with three rooms.

Today, guests may enjoy the wrap-around porch, the guest parlor with gold-leaf molding, Victorian furniture and a fabulous view, or the former library, now a family room. A third-floor refrigerator is stocked with free beverages.

Rooms and Rates: Seven - All on the second and third floors with queen beds, and light, contemporary Victorian decor. Bathrooms have clawfoot tubs with hand-held showers and pull chain toilets. Dr. Hancock's Room has a turret sitting area, marble tile floor in bathroom, done in yellow and green - $75. Florence's Room has white iron bed, turret sitting area, done in peach, green and white, private bath - $75. Master Bedroom has a carved oak headboard with lovebirds, done in blue and cream with Berber carpet - $75. Anna's Room has black iron bed, done in rose and white, dormer windows, private bath - $75. Doll Room has turret sitting area with wicker furniture, white iron and brass bed, done in light blue and white, shares bath with Train Room, which has gold iron bed, marble sink in room, done in yellow and cream - $55 each. Ballroom Suite has double whirlpool, done in burgundy and forest green - $125. Each additional person, $10. Rates are single or double. Add $20 for one-night rental of Saturday night only. Add tax.

Meals: Breakfast is served in the dining room at a time arranged the night before. It may include fresh seasonal fruit, fruit bread, egg and ham strata or pancakes, eggs and ham.

Dates Open: Year 'round

Smoking: Outside only

Children: Yes (crib available)

Pets: No

Handicapped Access: No

A/C: Window units

Other/Group Uses: No

Nearby: Fenelon Place Elevator, 8 blocks. Riverboat rides, 10 blocks. Greyhound track, 1.5 miles. Woodward Riverboat Museum, 10 blocks. Sundown Ski Area, 7 miles. Heritage Nature Trail, 4 miles. Downtown Galena, 14 miles.

Location: Take 12th up the bluff and turn left on Grove Terrace. Map sent.

Deposit: First night's lodging or confirmation by credit card

Payment: Cash, personal or traveler's checks, VISA or MasterCard

L'Auberge Mandolin

199 Loras
Dubuque, IA 52001
319-556-0069

Owner/Operator:
Judi Sinclair

Judi Sinclair did not make the decision lightly to move here, restore a home and open a B&B. A travel agent in L.A., "I had been looking into doing this for probably seven years," taking courses and reading books. But after looking on the West Coast, "I realized I was not going to get the size property I wanted there."

Although she "never was east of Des Moines in my life," Judi grew up visiting relatives in Iowa. In her work, she came across some impressive Dubuque tourism promotion and information about its architecture. So she sent for a phone book, and checked the shopping and numbers of plumbers and contractors. Finally, she contacted a realtor and toured historic homes. This was the last one on the list.

The home was built in 1908 by Nicholas Schrup, founder of an insurance company and five banks, including the still-family-owned American Trust and Savings Bank. It was donated by his two daughters as a convent for the nuns who ran the Catholic school around the corner. It once was a group home for troubled teens, and then was a lawyer's office and apartments.

It was rented mostly to college students when she bought it in January 1988. Removing dried bodies of aquarium fish from one room was among her tasks. To open in May, the parquet floors were refinished, four ceilings were replaced, bathrooms and a kitchen were added, plus total redecorating was completed.

The inn is named for the stained glass window by the oak staircase which has a woman holding a mandolin ("L'Auberge" means "the inn"). The wrap-around porch with a mosaic tile floor is open to guests, as are the parlors and dining room.

Rooms and Rates: Six - All on second or third floors. Grandmother's Room has queen brass and iron bed with quilt, antique toys - $65. Grant Tour Room has king bed with sink, decorated with European travel memorabilia; shares bath with tub only with Grandmother's Room - $65. Amanda's Room has collection of antique wedding photos, bay window, done in peach and green; bath has leaded glass windows, shower only - $75. Holly Marie's Room has bay window with bridge view, walnut furniture and wedding memorabilia, done in peach and green, bath with shower only - $80. Venetian Room is smaller room with queen brass and pewter bed, bath with shower only - $70. Third floor room has queen bed, wicker furniture, done in blue and white, bath with tub/shower - $80. Rates are single or double. Two-night minimum stay required summer weekends. Add tax.

Meals: Breakfast is served buffet-style in the dining room at 9. It may include fruit, a baked egg dish or cinnamon French toast with apricot sauce, muffins or cinnamon rolls.

Dates Open: Year 'round

Smoking: Outside only

Children: By special arrangement

Pets: No (little dog on premises)

Handicapped Access: No

A/C: Window units

Other/Group Uses: Meetings, private parties, teas, luncheons and dinners up to 12, bike tours.

Nearby: Fenelon Place Elevator, 10 blocks. Riverboat rides, 10 blocks. Greyhound track, 1.5 miles. Woodward Riverboat Museum, 10 blocks. Sundown Ski Area, 7 miles. Heritage Nature Trail, 4 miles. Downtown Galena, 14 miles.

Location: On the corner of Loras (same as 14th) and Main Street. Map sent.

Deposit: First night's lodging or confirmation by credit card

Payment: Cash, personal or traveler's checks, VISA or MasterCard

Redstone Inn

504 Bluff St.
Dubuque, IA 52001
319-582-1894

Owners/Operators:
Dubuque Historic Improvement Company
General Manager: Mary Moody

In 1894, Elizabeth Cooper married Dan Sullivan. Her father, A.A. Cooper, had arrived in Iowa in 1846 with just 25 cents to his name. But when Elizabeth married, he was a wealthy man, owning the Cooper Wagon Works, makers of prairie schooners. (One story says he was invited by Henry Ford to go into business making the horseless carriage, but told Ford his idea would never take, and Ford's effect on Detroit, not Dubuque, is history.)

Cooper was very concerned about his daughter's future. So, when he built Elizabeth a Victorian mansion for her wedding present, he designed it as a 27-room duplex so it could generate income in case her husband could not.

Ninety years later, 22 Dubuque investors spent nearly $1 million to buy, renovate, furnish and ultimately preserve the last of Cooper's mansions. Cooper's own 35-room residence already had been flattened into a parking lot. For years, the Redstone had been either apartments, a bar or vacant. The owners spent six months renovating and furnishing the mansion, on the National Register of Historic Places.

When the Redstone Inn opened in May 1985, it was a Victorian 15 guest-room inn with conveniences and elegance even Elizabeth Cooper never enjoyed. Mauve, burgundy, green and deep blue, which are in the Redstone's original stained glass windows, are used throughout the inn, as is polished woodwork and period antiques, all collected within 100 miles of Dubuque. Visitors register at an oak reception desk and choose rooms by seeing photos of each.

The elaborate parlor is available for use by guests. Bar service is available in the dining room or as room service.

Rooms and Rates: 15 - All have private baths, color TV, phones and individual thermostats controlling heat and air conditioning. Six rooms have whirlpools (with heavy robes provided), two with fireplaces. The huge Bridal Suite has hand-embroidered bedspread on queen bed, heart-shaped soaps, and, like the Governor's Suite and President's Suite, includes full breakfast, champagne, brandy, cheese and fruit tray - $165. Junior suites are smaller rooms with a whirlpool, include a continental breakfast - $125. Deluxe rooms - $88. Standard rooms - $69. Rates are single or double. Extra person over 12, $10. Cribs, $5. Packages available including riverboat rides, Victorian Progressive Dinner. Two-night minimum stay required on weekends. Add tax.

Meals: Breakfast is served in the dining room or to the guest room at 7-10 weekdays, 7-11 weekends. A full breakfast (egg dish, muffins, fruit) is included in the deluxe suite room rates. A continental breakfast (muffins or bagels, fruit) is included in the junior suite room rates. Breakfast is available to other guests and the general public.

Dates Open: Year 'round

Smoking: Yes

Children: Yes (cribs available)

Pets: No

Handicapped Access: No

A/C: Central

Other/Group Uses: Meetings, receptions, etc. handled at the Stout House.

Nearby: Fenelon Place Elevator, 2 blocks. Riverboat rides, 4 blocks. Greyhound tract, 1.5 miles. Woodward Riverboat Museum, 4 blocks. Sundown Ski Area, 7 miles. Heritage Nature Trail, 4 miles. Downtown Galena, 14 miles.

Location: Inn is on the corner of Fifth and Bluff.

Deposit: First night's lodging or confirmation by credit card

Payment: Cash, personal or traveler's checks, VISA, MasterCard or AMEX

The Richards House

1492 Locust St.
Dubuque, IA 52001
319-557-1492

Owner/Operator:
Dave Stuart
Innkeeper: Michelle Delaney

Benjamin Billings Richards was once connected with six Iowa banks, was a partner in the real estate business, and served 10 years in the Iowa Assembly. But it was his lumber connections that make this 1883 mansion so remarkable.

And don't judge this book by its cover — Dave Stuart has yet to restore the exterior. Inside are 11-1/2 foot ceilings, seven types of woodwork and 82 stained glass windows. The carved woodwork is ornate and unusual. In the dining room, above the built-in buffet are curved, leaded-glass mirrors, shaped in an arch to reflect the light from the gas chandeliers. The strips of wood decorating the ceiling are lined with a strip of brass. Even the house's four sets of pocket doors have stained-glass inserts.

The brick fireplace in the hallway says "Welcome." Other fireplaces have handpainted scenes from children's books or Upstate New York and the Adirondacks, where Richards grew up.

Stuart, who is in the Navy, purchased the house from the Richards family. B.B. Richards had the home built for his second wife, and he moved his in-laws next door into the four-story mansion. The widow of a grandson owned the National Register of Historic Places home until 1989, when Stuart opened the B&B. Luckily, the woodwork never was painted.

The first floor parlors, while sparsely furnished, have a TV and CD player for guests' use. Guests may also use the two back porches, one on the first floor and one on the second.

Rooms and Rates: Five - All with queen beds and terry robes. One suite has the bedroom in the former library, curtained off from the parlor, a new brass bed, fireplace, stained-glass window that says, "Choose your books as you choose your friends," dark cherry woodwork; half-bath in hall; shower upstairs - $70. On second floor: Yellow Room has handpainted fireplace, carved headboard, yellow striped wallpaper, bath with clawfoot tub/hand-held shower - $75. Green Room is done in green and white, shares bath back by servant's quarters with library downstairs (shower only) - $55. Blue Room has white iron bed, alcove sitting area, bath with clawfoot tub and handheld shower - $75. Rose Room has large floral print wallpaper, antique brass bed, bath with clawfoot tub/hand-held shower - $75. Rates are double; single, $10 less. Off-season, midweek discounts. Add tax.

Meals: Breakfast is served in the dining room 7:30-10:30. It may include fresh fruit, carrot or applesauce bread or coffeecake, buttermilk pancakes or waffles or three-grain pancakes, and sausage or bacon.

Dates Open: Year 'round

Children: Yes

Handicapped Access: No

Other/Group Uses: Parties up to 75

Smoking: Kitchen or porches only

Pets: "Sometimes"

A/C: Window units

Nearby: Fenelon Place Elevator, 11 blocks. Riverboat rides, 11 blocks. Greyhound track, 1.5 miles. Woodward Riverboat Museum, 11 blocks. Sundown Ski Area, 7 miles. Heritage Nature Trail, 4 miles. Downtown Galena, 14 miles.

Location: Located downtown at Locust and 15th. Map sent.

Deposit: First night's lodging or confirmation by credit card

Payment: Cash, personal or traveler's checks, VISA, MasterCard or AMEX

Stone Cliff Manor

195 W. 17th St. Owners/Operators:
Dubuque, IA 52001 Alice and Tc Ersepke
319-588-2856

Alice and Tc Ersepke, long-time collectors of antiques, have made this 16-room Queen Anne almost a museum. Every room is chock-full of Victorian furniture and art, with some collectibles for good measure. The library, for instance, has everything from a fainting couch to a coat of armor. The summer kitchen brims over with baskets, advertising memorabilia, a cast iron woodstove and other antiques, like an historical recreation at Michigan's Greenfield Village.

The home, located in Jackson Park Historic District, was built in 1889 by Charles Stampfer. He owned Stampfer Department Store, which was known around town as "the Macy's of Dubuque."

After being passed down to Stampfer's son, the home changed ownership several times and was converted into five apartments. Ersepkes removed four of them and opened the B&B in September 1987. "If you keep the apartments, you don't see that part of your home," Alice said.

Alice and Tc moved to Dubuque from Downers Grove, Ill., where they had restored an even older home. "We were going to Galena," Alice said, "but then we found the old homes in Dubuque." Alice is a nurse in Dubuque and Tc is retired. Daughter Heidi and two friendly dogs, Fritz and Lucy, share the home.

Upstairs, guests have use of a small art deco kitchen, and the refrigerator is stocked with beverages. A wicker screen porch has a gas grill. Guests may sit by the gas fireplace in the parlor or enjoy the library. Ersepkes are available to answer questions about their collections and give a home tour.

Rooms and Rates: Four - All with down comforters on double antique beds, color TVs and VCRs (movie tapes available), and private baths. Aunt Cora's Room is off the first-floor kitchen, bed with crocheted spread, decorated with Aunt Cora's vintage clothes, bath next door with shower and single whirlpool tub - $55. Victorian Suite is upstairs, bed set in alcove, electric reflecting fireplace, done in green and rose, bath with pull-chain toilet and clawfoot tub/shower - $75. Country Room has Amish clothes on the wall, electric brick fireplace, done in green and yellow, bath with clawfoot tub/shower - $75. Pollyanna room has collection of antique dolls, huge carved armoire from Paris, bath with clawfoot tub and separate marble shower - $75. Rates are single or double. Off-season, midweek and multiple night discounts. Tax included.

Meals: Breakfast is served in the dining room, to the guest room or on a screened porch at a time arranged the night before. It may include overnight French toast or light pancakes with fruit topping and cream, or steak and eggs.

Dates Open: Year 'round

Children: "Well-behaved"

Handicapped Access: No

Smoking: "Discouraged"

Pets: No (two dogs on premises)

A/C: Window units

Other/Group Uses: Teas, meetings, socials, breakfasts or luncheons up to 15 people.

Nearby: Fenelon Place Elevator, 13 blocks. Riverboat rides, 13 blocks. Greyhound track, 1.5 miles. Woodward Riverboat Museum, 13 blocks. Sundown Ski Area, 7 miles. Heritage Nature Trail, 4 miles. Downtown Galena, 14 miles.

Location: On the corner of 17th and Main. Map sent.

Deposit: $25 per room per night

Payment: Cash, personal or traveler's checks only

The Stout House

11th and Locust
Dubuque, IA 52001
319-582-1894

Owners/Operators:
Dubuque Historic Improvement Company
General Manager: Mary Moody

After 22 investors formed the Dubuque Historic Improvement Company to buy Elizabeth Cooper's home and open the Redstone Inn, they decided to do it again. This time, the structure is another red sandstone mansion six blocks away. After renovation, the doors to a five-room B&B opened in May 1986 in the Frank D. Stout house.

Built in 1890-91, the $75,000 home served as a grand place for the president of the Knapp Stout Lumber Company to entertain and to raise his five children with Clara, his wife. In 1901, Stout moved to Chicago, and died in 1927 as one of Chicago's 10 wealthiest men, having also been a railroad and electric company president and having owned timber in the South and West.

In 1911, after a few other owners, the Archdiocese of Dubuque bought it as its office headquarters and home for the Archbishop, and operated it as such for nearly 75 years.

Today, guests check in at the reception hall, paneled in rosewood. The library is open for guests' use, where they can read by a green onyx fireplace. Rolltop bookcases are built in to the walls, and onyx and mosaics are used in several places.

Like the Redstone Inn, this house has been furnished with period furniture, all obtained within 100 miles of Dubuque. Some original furnishings remain, like the grandfather clock in the reception hall and the stained-glass windows. Unlike the Redstone Inn, this building was kept almost in original condition by its previous owners.

A second-floor lounge has a color TV and phone for guests' use.

Rooms and Rates: Five - All upstairs, done in antiques and brass beds. Room #21 has double bed with Italian marble bath with tub only - $100. Rooms #22 and #23 have queens beds, share Italian marble bath with tub/shower - $85. Rooms #25 and #26 have queen beds, share a bath with tub/shower - $85. Rates are single or double. Extra person over 12, $10. Cribs, $5. Two-night minimum stay required weekends. Add tax.

Meals: Continental breakfast is served in the dining room 8-10. It may include homemade muffins or cinnamon rolls, fresh fruit and cold cereal.

Dates Open: Year 'round

Smoking: Yes

Children: Yes (cribs available)

Pets: No

Handicapped Access: No

A/C: Window units in guest rooms

Other/Group Uses: Meetings, parties, receptions catered to 100.

Nearby: Fenelon Place Elevator, 7 blocks. Riverboat rides, 9 blocks. Greyhound track, 1.5 miles. Woodward Riverboat Museum, 9 blocks. Sundown Ski Area, 7 miles. Heritage Nature Trail, 4 miles. Downtown Galena, 14 miles.

Location: On the corner of 11th and Bluff.

Deposit: First night's lodging or confirmation by credit card

Payment: Cash, personal or traveler's checks, VISA, MasterCard or AMEX

Captain Merry Guest House

399 Sinsinawa Ave.
East Dubuque, IL 61025
815-747-3644

Owners/Operators:
Madi and Joe Schlarman

It's not documented fact that Abe Lincoln danced with a Dubuque woman in this home, but it's widely believed that Al Capone stayed in this house. "He came here when things got hot in Chicago," said Madi Schlarman. East Dubuque, which remained "wet" as long as possible during Prohibition, was known as "Sin City."

The Merry House, built in 1857 by Captain Charles Hamilton Merry, had unusual limestone tunnels built from the basement, one of which was a canal (when the house was built, the Mississippi was undammed and all that came between it and the house was a limestone retaining wall). Local stories say that when gamblers were about to be raided, the equipment would be tunneled here. Merry owned the ferry crossing the river, a granary and possibly part of a railroad.

When Schlarmans bought this home in 1983, "there were rats in the basement and pigeons in the attic," Madi said. Windows were missing. Fixtures had been stolen. The slate roof had leaked from the belvedere to the basement. Yet it was one of few river homes to have indoor plumbing and central heating, and a home worth saving, they decided. And they had the talented family to do it.

Joe, who "retired" into this house project, Madi, a nurse, and their three adult children worked for more than five years on this house, Joe doing so full-time. One son was the electrician, another made the plaster moldings throughout the house; daughter Julie designed stencils and stenciled rooms, and did research.

Guests are welcome to use the dining room and parlor with piano. They also may climb to the third floor belvedere for views, and they get a guided tour of the basement, its tunnel and its "dungeon."

Rooms and Rates: Five - All upstairs with double beds, pine plank floors with oriental rugs, painted and stenciled rooms with cream or white-colored woodwork and moldings. All share a bath with clawfoot tub/shower and two pedestal sinks. Captain's Room is done in rose and cream, has Victorian brocade drapes - $50. Sarah's Room has blue and white decor, large white stencil pattern - $50. The Children's Room has unusual curved, pressed maple bed, tulip and heart stencil pattern, Priscilla curtains, done in rose and green - $50. Eliza's Room has carved bed, done in yellow, burgundy and blue - $40. Pink Room is the former nursery, has toy motif, white plank floors - $40. Rates are single or double. Off-season rates. Add tax.

Meals: Breakfast is served in the dining room at a time arranged the night before. It may include fruit compote, egg strata, locally-made sausage and muffins, or potato pancakes, bratwurst and scrambled eggs.

Dates Open: Year 'round

Smoking: In kitchen where owners do

Children: "By special arrangment"

Pets: No (dog and cat in owner's quarters)

Handicapped Access: No

A/C: Central (four units, in fact)

Other/Group Uses: No

Nearby: Restaurants, marina in East Dubuque. Downtown Dubuque, just across the bridge (1/2 mile). Downtown Galena, 14 miles.

Location: The B&B is pink and you'll see it from the Highway 20 bridge coming from Dubuque. From Highway 20 going into Dubuque from Galena, continue toward bridge. Home is on the right before the bridge. Map sent.

Deposit: $10 or confirmation by credit card

Payment: Cash, personal or traveler's checks, VISA or MasterCard

Juniper Hill Farm

15325 Budd Road
Dubuque, IA 52001
319-582-4405

Owners/Operators:
Ruth and Bill McEllhiney

In 1848, as allowed under the Iowa Homestead Act, John Morgan purchased these 40 acres for $20 (the abstract was signed by President Zachary Taylor). Morgan homesteaded with a mule. The old Dubuque-Colesburg-Decorah stagecoach route came through here, and some wagon wheel ruts are still visible.

One day in 1987, Bill McEllhiney came home and announced he had bought the farm. "We had a gorgeous house in town," said Ruth about the surprise. "We were all mad because we couldn't figure out what he'd do with it!" Their grown children, Bill said, "thought their dad had lost it." The house, Ruth said, "had gone to rack and ruin." It took a year just to clear dead junipers from the property.

But Bill, who retired from his well drilling business, wanted to be close to the Sundown Ski Area. McEllhineys had been one of 10 founding families of the slope. And the view, which, on a clear day, stretches 28 miles to Platteville, Wis., captivated him. Plus, he admits, he had a B&B in the back of his mind.

An architect was hired to design added space. Original pine paneling was whitewashed for a lighter, country look. Rooms with private baths and skylights and a sunny dining room were added. Bill talked Ruth into selling the Dubuque house, and McEllhineys have plenty of space in half the house. Until Ruth retires from her claims supervisor job at John Deere Insurance, Bill handles B&B duties.

When "Field of Dreams" was filmed in nearby Dyersville, art director Leslie McDonald lived here. She left food for a cast-off Sheltie and enticed him down to the farm. Now named "Shoeless Joe" for the name of the book on which the film was based, the dog has become McEllhineys' full-time farm dog.

Guests have a common room with bay window, brick fireplace, 1900s cast iron stove and color TV. Appetizers and beverages are served there in the afternoon.

Rooms and Rates: Three - All with whitewashed wainscoted walls, carpet and Iowa Mennonite quilts. Honeymoon Suite has queen spindle bed with heart quilt, white wicker furniture, bath with double whirlpool, separate shower - $85. Peach Room has two double beds with double wedding ring quilts, bath with shower only - $85. Yellow Room has two twin spool beds, done in light yellow and green, view of walking trail in woods, private bath across hall with shower only - $65. Rates are single or double. Each additional adult, $20. Business and multiple night stay discounts. Two-night minimum stay required weekends. Tax included.

Meals: Breakfast is served in the common room at a time arranged the night before. It may include banana-raspberry slushes, homemade raisin bran muffins with honey butter, warm fruit compote on phyllo dough, and ham and egg casserole, omelettes, Belgian waffles or pancakes.

Dates Open: Year 'round

Smoking: In common room only

Children: "Well supervised"

Pets: No (outdoor pets on premises)

Handicapped Access: No

A/C: Central

Other/Group Uses: Meetings and retreats up to 20, small outdoor weddings.

Nearby: Pond fishing, hiking, bird watching, x-c skiing, ice skating on premises. Sundown Ski Area, behind B&B. Heritage Trail, within 1 mile. Downtown Dubuque, 8 miles. Downtown Galena, 22 miles.

Location: West on Highway 20 through Dubuque. Go to Asbury. Map sent.

Deposit: First night's lodging or confirmation by credit card

Payment: Cash, personal or traveler's checks, VISA or MasterCard

Oak Crest Cottage

9866 Military Road
Dubuque, IA 52001
319-582-4207

Owners/Operators:
Barb and Jerry Hawbaker

Right after Barb and Jerry Hawbaker opened their restored cottage, not one, but two, movie stars were guests. Amy Madigan, who starred as Kevin Costner's wife in "Field of Dreams," stayed for nearly three months while filming the movie in 1988. Madigan's husband, actor Ed Harris ("The Abyss" and he starred as John Glenn in "The Right Stuff"), also made it his home for a month.

"They joined us for our annual Fourth of July family picnic," Barb said. "That's one reunion they'll *never* forget," she said of her family.

This cottage, aptly named, was built on a blufftop by William Canfield, Jr., owner of the 250-room Canfield Hotel downtown (the first air-conditioned hotel in Iowa). Canfield used it as his second home. He leased the land, but liked it so well he bought it and built a larger home later on the site, where Hawbakers now live.

But the cottage suffered during a succession of owners. "When we moved here, it was either tear it down or fix it up," Barb said. They had new plumbing and wiring put in, then tackled the rest of the work themselves. Barb is a furniture saleswoman and Jerry is a project engineer for John Deere, so work went on weekends and evenings for more than 18 months.

"It was really primitive." Walls were stripped to lathe, and Hawbakers found that cardboard boxes from the hotel kitchen had been used as insulation. They rebuilt the foundation, insulated, sanded floors, removed plywood paneling, moved knotty pine paneling to the ceiling, enlarged windows and put in a full kitchen. Upstairs, they added a bath, took out a ladder and put in a staircase, and improved the bedrooms. Barb wallpapered and sewed cafe curtains.

Guests have a large limestone fireplace in the living area and color TV. They are free to walk a nature trail and explore the six acres. The front porch has wicker furniture and a view from the bluff.

Rooms and Rates: Private cottage with two upstairs bedrooms off a loft balcony, one with double bed, done in peach and beige, one with twin beds, done in rose and cream. Bath upstairs has tub only. Bath downstairs has shower only. Downstairs, full kitchen also has dishwasher. Queen country sofa sleeper, rag rug in front of large limestone fireplace, dining table, wing chairs. $60 weekdays, $75 weekends for one couple; $105 weekdays, $125 weekends for two couples; $130 and $150 for three couples. Two-night minimum stay required weekends. Add tax.

114

Meals: Cook-your-own in complete kitchen with coffee maker, coffee, filters. Staples are supplied in cupboards and refrigerator.

Dates Open: Year 'round

Smoking: Yes

Children: Welcome

Pets: Outdoor kennel available

Handicapped Access: No

A/C: Central

Other/Group Uses: Meetings and retreats up to 15, weddings up to 30.

Nearby: Swiss Valley Park and Nature Center (hiking, x-c ski trails, interpretive center), 3 miles. E.B. Lyon's Nature Center, including Mines of Spain area, 3 miles. St. Donatus (antiquing, doll museum, Way of the Cross, bakery), 10 miles. Downtown Dubuque, 7 miles. Downtown Galena, 21 miles.

Location: Highway 61 south to light past Highway 52 intersection. Map sent.

Deposit: One night's lodging or half of entire stay

Payment: Cash, personal or traveler's checks only

Contents Grouped By Category*

B&B: **Page:**

*Please note that these categories are regardless of legal definition and were assigned by the author, who is fully aware that someone, somewhere is going to strongly disagree. Some decisions are arguable, so please read the full descriptions and definitions in the introduction, then decide for yourself. Briefly, B&Bs usually have only a few guest rooms, and guests feel like they are staying in someone's home and have a chance to sit and visit with the host(s). Country inns usually are larger and more private with possibly more amenities, but sometimes at the expense of contact with the innkeepers, who may have separate quarters. Read the full descriptions carefully to make sure you will get the type of experience you want.

Private Apartments/Suites Available: **Page:**

Located on Farms (guests can hike on property):   **Page:**

Exceptional view property: **Page:**

Whirlpool rooms or hot tubs on the premises: **Page:**

     *Construction not completed as of this writing

Woodburning fireplace rooms:*   **Page:**
     *Working fireplaces are not allowed in guest rooms of B&Bs within Galena city limits (many inns have fireplaces in parlors or other common rooms)

Traveling to Galena B&Bs?

To help plan your visit to the Galena area, more information is available from the Galena/Jo Daviess County Convention and Visitors Bureau.

For a "fat packet" of free literature, call toll-free **1-800-747-9377** between 9 a.m. and 5 p.m. seven days a week.

The packet includes information on events, lodging, restaurants, outdoor recreation, antique shops, historic sites, art galleries, and a county map. It also has coupons good for discounts on weeknight stays at a variety of B&Bs and other lodging facilities.

In addition, the person who answers your call will be able to answer your questions about room availability on busy weekends.

To write or visit the main information office (located in the restored Galena Depot):
Galena/Jo Daviess County Convention and Visitors Bureau
101 Bouthillier St.
Galena, IL 61036
(815-777-0203)

GALENA / JO DAVIESS COUNTY
CONVENTION & VISITORS BUREAU

Traveling to Dubuque B&Bs?

More information about what to see and do, where to eat, and seasonal events is available from the Dubuque Convention and Visitors Bureau.

For a copy of the Dubuque Visitor's Guide, call toll-free **1-800-79-VISIT (1-800-798-4748)** between 9 a.m. and 5 p.m. seven days a week.

The guide includes information on 27 popular attractions, annual events, parks, outdoor recreation and shopping. It also has downtown and area maps and a list of historic buildings in the area.

During the summer, the Bureau also can answer your questions about room availability on busy weekends.

To write or visit the travel information office:
>Dubuque Convention and Visitors Bureau
>770 Town Clock Plaza
>Dubuque, IA 52001
>(319-557-9200)

or

>Tourist Information Center
>Dodge and Locust
>Dubuque, IA 52001
>(319-556-4372)

This picture of what is now the Aldrich Guest House, 900 Third St., was
taken sometime after the 1880s, when a second major addition was made to
what originally was a one-room house. The Aldrich Guest House is featured
on pages 28-29. (Photo courtesy of the Alfred W. Mueller Collection,
Illinois Historic Preservation Agency)

Mrs. Lucretia Snyder and daughters Fanny and Alice enjoyed the porch at 1000 Third St., now Comfort Guest House, on pages 38-39. (Photo courtesy of the Alfred W. Mueller Collection, Illinois Historic Preservation Agency)

The Hellman mansion, 318 Hill St., is pictured when Hellmans owned it, 1895 to 1922. Hellman Guest House is on pages 58-59. (Photo courtesy of the Alfred W. Mueller Collection, Illinois Historic Preservation Agency)

Want to be a Field Editor?

I'm often told that if I need help researching these books, I'd have no shortage of volunteers. Well, consider this your chance.

As the number of B&Bs and inns in the Galena Area grows, I could use the comments of a few good travelers. (Same goes for all of Wisconsin and Minnesota, where I also publish "Room at the Inn" guidebooks.)

Know of an historic B&B or inn that should be included in the next edition? Did you stay at one that wasn't up to snuff and should be left out? Or, worst of all, did you find mistakes in this edition or information that has changed?

I'd also like to know if this book was helpful to you or how to make it more so, or of bookstores and gift shops that aren't carrying it, but should. (Better yet, tell *them!*)

Your first-person feedback is welcome. Write to me at:
Down to Earth Publications
1426 Sheldon
St. Paul, MN 55108

Please make sure you include the **name and address of the B&B or inn visited, dates of your visit,** and **your name and address.** And please be **specific** in whatever information you provide. Also, I may share your ideas with innkeepers, so please note if you do not want your name or comments used.

Thank you!

Laura

**Order
by
post**

Copies of **Room at the Inn/Galena Area** are available by mail.
Cost: $7.95 retail, plus $2.00 postage, handling and tax = $9.95

Traveling to Wisconsin? **Room at the Inn/Wisconsin** features 112 select
inns throughout the state in the same format. 288 pages.
Cost: $12.95 retail, plus $2.00 postage, handling and tax = $14.95

Minnesota's historic B&Bs are featured in **Room at the Inn/Minnesota**, a
guide to 60 historic B&Bs, hotels and country inns, plus 17 contemporary inns.
Cost: $9.95 retail, plus $2.00 postage, handling and tax = $11.95

"WAKE UP & SMELL THE COFFEE - Upper Midwest Edition"
contains 180+ recipes from 86 B&Bs in Illinois, Iowa, Minnesota, Wisconsin and
Michigan. (Pacific Northwest edition due out Fall '90 - $11.95; by mail, $13.95.)
Cost: $14.95 retail, plus $2.00 postage, handling and tax = $16.95

Additional copies may be ordered from:
   Down to Earth Publications
   1426 Sheldon
   St. Paul, MN 55108.
Please make checks payable to Down to Earth Publications. Books are mailed
special fourth class rate. Please allow a few weeks for delivery.

Or charge it with V/MC at **1-800-888-9653.**

Travel Notes

**Order
by
post**

Copies of **Room at the Inn/Galena Area** are available by mail.
    Cost: $7.95 retail, plus $2.00 postage, handling and tax = $9.95

Traveling to Wisconsin? **Room at the Inn/Wisconsin** features 112 select
inns throughout the state in the same format. 288 pages.
    Cost: $12.95 retail, plus $2.00 postage, handling and tax = $14.95

Minnesota's historic B&Bs are featured in **Room at the Inn/Minnesota,** a
guide to 60 historic B&Bs, hotels and country inns, plus 17 contemporary inns.
    Cost: $9.95 retail, plus $2.00 postage, handling and tax = $11.95

"WAKE UP & SMELL THE COFFEE - Upper Midwest Edition"
contains 180+ recipes from 86 B&Bs in Illinois, Iowa, Minnesota, Wisconsin and
Michigan. (Pacific Northwest edition due out Fall '90 - $11.95; by mail, $13.95.)
    Cost: $14.95 retail, plus $2.00 postage, handling and tax = $16.95

Additional copies may be ordered from:
    Down to Earth Publications
    1426 Sheldon
    St. Paul, MN 55108.
Please make checks payable to Down to Earth Publications. Books are mailed
special fourth class rate. Please allow a few weeks for delivery.

Or charge it with V/MC at **1-800-888-9653.**

About the author

Laura Zahn is president of Down to Earth Publications, a St. Paul, Minnesota, writing, publishing and public relations firm specializing in travel. Her travelwriting has appeared in many newspapers and magazines.

Her first book was just plain "Room at the Inn: Guide to Historic B&Bs, Hotels and Country Inns Close to the Twin Cities" in 1986. It is out of print and has been replaced by **"Room at the Inn/Minnesota," "Room at the Inn/Wisconsin,"** and now **"Room at the Inn/Galena Area."**

In October 1988, Zahn published **"WAKE UP & SMELL THE COFFEE - Upper Midwest Edition,"** a collection of breakfast, brunch and other favorite recipes from small B&Bs in Wisconsin, Minnesota, Michigan, Illinois and Iowa. In these Upper Midwest B&Bs, guests literally can wake up and smell breakfast cooking. The **"Pacific Northwest Edition"** is due out in Fall 1990 and will include recipes from B&Bs in Washington and Oregon.

Zahn also co-wrote "Ride Guide to the Historic Alaska Railroad."

Zahn shares her St. Paul home with Jim Miller, her geologist husband, and Kirby Puckett Zahn Miller, who was proudly adopted from the Humane Society of Ramsey County on the day the Minnesota Twins won the American League pennant in 1987. Both help with the publishing business: Jim makes the maps for all of the books and gives advice and support, and Kirby never fails to announce the arrival of the day's mail.